My VIRGIN KITCHEN

My VIRGIN KITCHEN

Delicious recipes you can make every day

BARRY LEWIS

HarperCollins*Publishers*

THIS BOOK IS DEDICATED TO EVERYONE THAT HAS SUPPORTED ME
IN THIS JOURNEY – THANK YOU SO MUCH FOR MAKING IT POSSIBLE

HarperCollinsPublishers
1 London Bridge Street
London SE1 9GF

www.harpercollins.co.uk

First published by HarperCollinsPublishers 2017

10 9 8 7 6 5 4 3 2 1

A catalogue record of this book is available from the British Library

ISBN 978-0-00-754479-0

Printed and bound in China

CONTENTS

INTRODUCTION

Welcome to My Virgin Kitchen

Growing up I always had a fascination for food. I was never really afraid to try new things, but when it came to cooking I had very little exposure to it; sure, I licked the bowl when making cakes with my mother and, despite being awful at home economics at school, I did really enjoy trying to cook. I also enjoyed TV cookery shows and found them quite soothing to watch – my hero when I was younger was Keith Floyd. I loved his casual approach to cooking and the way he told the cameraman what to do. Those were also the days of classic TV chefs such as Delia, Gary Rhodes (loved his spiky hair) and good ol' Ainsley Harriott and co in *Ready Steady Cook*. Then giants like Gordon Ramsay and Jamie Oliver burst on to the scene and took TV cooking up a notch. As I've said before, it was really Jamie Oliver who inspired me to pick up a camera. After watching him poach an egg as part of a more complex dish where he just pretty much threw the egg into the water, I was inspired to give food vlogging a go and MyVirginKitchen was born.

You see, when it came to the kitchen I *was* a virgin, a self-taught chap just having a go. I had no idea what I was really doing and not just when it came to the cooking – I'm talking about the filming, editing, presenting and all that goes with it. But that first poached egg I filmed worked; I had a couple of nice comments and things just rolled on from there. I found that rather than just inspiring myself, I was beginning to inspire others, too. I realised it was becoming a passion: the fear had gone and I'd fallen in love with the world of food. I started to make sacrifices, like giving up football or tennis, and focused more on putting out content. It brought my daughter Phoebe and me together – laughing and having fun in the kitchen – but learning, too. Instead of running around a football pitch I was making flapjacks with her and I loved it. My second daughter Chloe has grown up with a daddy who 'does cooking videos on the internet'. Things evolved fast and now my wife, Becky (aka Mrs Barry), is part of this crazy world of vlogging, appearing whenever she can as well! It's been an insanely crazy journey to date; if I'm honest it still just feels like one big day stitched together. But I'm going with the flow and would still do videos even if I had my old job. Cooking is simply what I do now and I love it.

People sometimes refer to me as a chef: I need to state categorically that I am not a chef of any sort. I'm just a self-taught cook who wants to inspire people to get into the kitchen, have some fun, make some great food, laugh and learn. That's all there is to it. To me, cooking is about embracing the fun moments, the adventure, the unknown and the gastronomic playground that is your kitchen! My technique for inspiring you is to make you smile. So what if you make a cake and get a little flour over you, or a little eggshell in the mix? No one is perfect, so embrace the fun, the laughter and the chaos in the kitchen.

Day by day I've learned new techniques, cooking styles, hints and tips, and tried hundreds of recipes – a lot of the ideas have come from you guys. I'm immensely proud of bringing some of my best ideas to life in this book and cannot wait to see you all getting stuck in and sharing your attempts.

Each chapter has its own introduction, but I feel it's pretty important to say why each chapter is there and what you can get from it:

FEEL-GOOD RECIPES

In this section you will find a real variety of lighter bites and recipes that make you feel good. As with so many of the recipes in this book, many of them are vegetarian or can be adjusted accordingly. Sometimes a slightly lighter meal or one that makes you feel good is just what the doctor ordered. This chapter is a really great way to kick off the book.

KIDS' CORNER

As the title suggests, this chapter is about showcasing lots of recipes to cook with and for kids. There's a good balance of inspiration here between recipes that the kids can pretty much do by themselves (maybe with a little help or guidance) and dishes to get them eating food in a fun way, often presenting it differently or exposing them to different flavours.

TASTE OF THE WORLD

These recipes are inspired by dishes from all round the world. Many of these are my spin on ideas that have been shared with me online, some of which I had never heard of before. Of course, nothing can quite beat eating foods from round the world in their original countries, but this is my way of showcasing some different styles and concepts without having to hop on a plane! The Pizza Parlour is the place to start your own pizzeria at home with some hints, tips, recipes and suggestions based around five unique pizzas, including a gorgeous sweet potato base version. Mix and match your toppings here and be sure to let me know how you get on.

NOSTALGIC RECIPES

On a personal level, this is about winding back the clock for me. There are several moments in my life from which the food memories are so vivid; eating those dishes always triggers my taste buds and my memories. The Chicken Thigh Parmigiana (see page 114) is a great starting point – it's absolutely delicious. Food really does create memories and hopefully some of the recipes in the book will become memorable for you, too.

TWISTS ON CLASSICS

For me, putting a spin on traditional dishes is like thinking outside the box. I really enjoy experimenting with different concepts and breaking the norm; I could have easily written a whole book on this topic alone! There's something for everyone in this section and don't forget: you can always put your own twists on these twists too and take them to another level!

BAKES & CAKES

A huge serving of delicious desserts for you right here, with lots of lovely flavour combinations going on. There are some gorgeous cakes along with some pretty simple (but impressive) puds, too; try the No-bake Bounty Tart (see page 170). I'm confident this chapter will get a fair bit of usage!

So, what do I want you to get from this book? I just want to make the point that it is really a guide. I want you in that kitchen getting stuck into the recipes and learning for yourself – what works for me may not work for someone else. If you're not keen on an ingredient (or don't have it to hand), tweak the recipe. I love personalising recipes and want you to do the same, then share, share, share! I'm on most social media platforms and the most awesome thing is seeing you guys getting into the kitchen. I'm regularly sent pictures of fellow kitchen virgins giving something a go, kids cooking with their parents or even established cooks and chefs shaking it up with some new ideas. We've got a little community going on and now you have bought this book you are part of it too!

Right then, what are you waiting for? Get exploring the pages, mark out some favourites, grab the ingredients and get in that kitchen! Good luck!

GETTING KIDS AROUND THE TABLE

One thing I am asked quite often by fellow parents online is: do I have any fun ideas or ways to get kids excited about mealtimes? My children have grown up seeing me getting excited about food and obviously had quite a big involvement in the kitchen so I think it's natural that they've just begun to love it too.

I firmly believe that by just getting the family around the table you are halfway there. It's too easy these days for them to be distracted by other things, from cartoons to phones and tablets. Have a look at the ideas listed below (some of which form part of the kids' cooking chapter) and work out which ones you could use to get your kids excited about food. And if you have any of your own you'd like to share, do reach out to me on social media – I'm always keen to learn more.

☐ GET THEM TO MAKE IT THEMSELVES

This is a pretty obvious one and an idea that is pushed hard throughout this book. Start with foods you know they'll like (fajitas and pizzas are a fantastic way of easing them into the world of food) and embrace the kitchen chaos. Let them laugh and learn and they'll be showing off their meal creations in no time.

☐ HIDE THE VEG

Hiding vegetables in other ingredients is having a bit of a comeback. My Nan used to do it all the time, particularly with parsnips! A couple of recipes in the book explore this idea, such as the Hidden Vegetable Pasta Bake (see page 66) or Honey Mustard Chicken with Spinach Mash (see page 48). Root vegetables such as swede or parsnip can easily be hidden in mashed potato. Just be sure to let your kids finish the dish before revealing what is actually in it!

☐ MINI FOOD

Making miniature portions of foods can be a really fun thing to do – it makes things much more visually exciting for the kids. I've lost count of the number of times I've made tiny plates of spaghetti bolognese (including a tiny one for Barbie) for the kids to try. It is actually pretty good fun for adults too, so if you want a little kids' tea party with a difference, give it a try. There's plenty of inspiration on my website for mini foods, but it can just be a case of making a standard portion and serving it on teeny plates!

☐ COLOURFUL MEALS

I must be a big kid too because I fall for this one often. There's something about colour that really draws you into a dish. Our kids are fascinated if we make something brightly coloured – if you call it a 'rainbow' you are almost guaranteed to hook their attention. Try making a rainbow pizza, for example, with red onion, peppers, courgettes, cheese and tomato to create a cool topping effect.

DIFFERENT PASTA SHAPES

Shapes as well as colours are a very appealing to children – remember those smiley potato faces or alphabet oven chips? Well, they are popular for a reason, but you can create the same fun effect with some homemade pasta and cookie cutters in cool shapes. Ever seen train-shaped ravioli? Get the cutters out and try the Crab Ravioli (see page 60).

MEALS ON A STICK

Put something on a stick and no longer is it just a dinner, it's the most 'exciting thing to ever happen to dinner time' (to quote Phoebe). Yep, sometimes all you need is a good old bamboo skewer to get the kids gobbling up their food. You'd be surprised what you can put on a stick – the Caprese Chicken Salad (see page 25) works a charm. And if you're still struggling, just call them lollipops – that always seems to seal the deal.

HEALTHIER TWISTS

This one is a bit of a mind game. Of course, children are often drawn to less healthy snacks, be that through the media, convenience or just cravings. Use this to your advantage by making these naughtier snacks a little healthier. I once made a homemade 'Happy Meal' with my children and nephews using smoothie, cornflake-baked chicken nuggets (as seen in my first book) and baked sweet potato fries. It went down a storm – because I told them it was a homemade 'Happy Meal', they went bonkers for it. Making

healthy versions of crisps, such as baked apple crisps or banana chips is also a smart move.

CHARACTER CAKES AND FUNNY FACES

You don't have to wait for the next birthday party to make a Minion cake! And I've found that recreating funny faces or characters on the dinner plate can work fantastically. For example, make a chilli but use the rice to make funny hair, and soured cream blobs, cheese and herbs for facial expressions. I'm sure that Cookie Monster Cupcakes (see my website) get eaten twice as fast as standard ones in our house, but try to be creative with the savoury stuff too.

BOARD GAME PLATE

I've not actually tried this yet, but we went to a children's party where the food was served on paper plates that had squares drawn on them. Each square had a separate portion of food in it with a start and end. The idea was that you followed the squares clockwise until you got to the final one – a piece of cake! I thought that was a pretty neat way of making eating food fun.

ICE-CUBE TRAY

Take an ice-cube tray and portion the dinner into each little slot; it may look a bit strange, but suddenly that huge intimidating plate of food becomes bite-size and manageable. Work with your kids here if they are always keen to hop away from the table before finishing a meal, and remember that you don't have to fill up all the slots. This has worked a charm for us, particularly when introducing new foods.

MY TOP 4 KITCHEN TIPS

READ RECIPE BEFORE ATTEMPTING IT

It took me a while to work this one out, but it really is useful. It's tempting to just look at the ingredients needed in a recipe and crack on one step at a time, but taking the time to read the full method can give you a much better understanding of the finished dish and what is involved. It will also enable you to put your own spin on things, which for me is what cooking is all about – personalisation. Having the confidence and understanding the full story before you start a recipe will make life so much easier.

KEEP YOUR KNIVES SHARP

This is quite an obvious one and you've probably heard it before, but a blunt knife can give you poorly cut food, slow you down and – most importantly – it is dangerous. Invest in a decent knife sharpener; there's something very satisfying about prepping food with a sharp knife. No matter how fast or slow you are when it comes to slicing, your fingers will thank you for it!

PREP LIKE YOU'RE ON A COOKING SHOW

When I'm filming I always have my ingredients ready and laid out before attempting a recipe, but even when I'm not filming and am just cooking at home for the family I still find it beneficial. It's worth getting a nice little collection of small food prep bowls that you can stack after each ingredient is used; anything that will take the hassle out of the steps so you are fully prepared and can concentrate on the good stuff is good in my book.

USE EGGSHELL TO REMOVE SHELL

In the early years of MyVirginKitchen, whenever we cracked eggs into a bowl both Phoebe and I would quite often end up with a little eggshell floating in the bowl. I'd be trying to scoop it out with my fingers – if you've ever done this you'll know it can take ages to fish out! A great little tip is to take a large piece of eggshell and scoop it into the bowl – the smaller piece of shell will cling to it. Try it – it works a charm!

SOME OF MY FAVOURITE KITCHEN UTENSILS

SILICONE SPATULA

My favourite kitchen utensil ever. I love a good wooden spoon when it comes to mixing but there is no greater satisfaction than scraping a bowl clean in one good swoop with a spatula!

TONGS

Love tongs! I look at them as being like a giant finger and thumb that you can use to manipulate your food, allowing you to flip, spin and grab most items of food safely. A well-known chef (who shall remain nameless) actually pinched my favourite pair at a food festival! Obviously a fan too.

FOOD SCISSORS

Yep, having a decent set of kitchen scissors in your drawer can be a lifesaver in certain circumstances. Obviously useful for opening cartons and packets, but I also use them for roughly cutting up bunches of fresh herbs, or even slicing chicken portions, sausages or bacon into smaller pieces. If I can use scissors instead of a knife, I will!

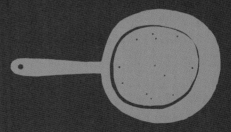

DECENT NON-STICK PANS

I used to have quite a cheap set of pans but I soon realised what a difference a decent set makes. Like all pans they have a shelf life and you need to treat them right, but a good set of non-stick pans in a few sizes can make the whole cooking experience so much easier.

TOP 5 KITCHEN FAIL SOLUTIONS

CAKE RISES UP IN THE MIDDLE

I have found spreading the batter to the outer edges of the cake tin with a palette knife can prevent this happening most of the time. If it does still happen, use a long, serrated knife to carefully slice off the top once cooled, especially if the final cake is being covered in icing and decorated.

PASTRY DOESN'T ROLL OUT/BREAKS

Whether you're using homemade or shop-bought pastry it's important to chill it in the fridge until needed, but you'll need to take it out of the fridge to bring to room temperature before working with it. Adding too much flour when you are rolling out will affect the consistency of the pastry, so avoid this by rolling the pastry between two sheets of baking parchment; this also makes it less messy, too!

BURNT BOTTOM OF SAUCEPAN

I get this a lot! In fact it happens to everyone I'm sure; there's nothing worse than trying to scrub the bottom of a burnt pan. The best solution I've found? Add water with a few squirts of washing-up liquid to the pan and place it back over the heat. Bring to the boil, letting it simmer for around 5 minutes. Remove from the heat, pour out the water and scrub with a wire cloth or silicone spatula.

CASSEROLE IS TOO THICK/THIN

If something is too thick adding extra water, stock or other liquid usually does the trick. In terms of thickening a recipe adding cornflour (mixed with a little water first into a paste) works, as does adding cooked grains or pulses or even breadcrumbs.

OOPS, MY RECIPE IS TOO SPICY

Sometimes a blob of soured cream just won't cut it to cool things down! If it's a beef chilli, for example, fry some extra beef mince and add to the dish to spread out the flavour. Another trick is to add sugar, particularly to casseroles or soups. Just add very small pinches and keep tasting until you are happy.

10 TERMS USED IN THIS BOOK

BLIND BAKE

To bake something (usually pastry) before you add the filling to prevent the pastry becoming soggy on the bottom.

CREAM

To mix ingredients (usually butter and sugar) together to achieve a smooth, creamy finish.

WHIP/WHISK

To use a hand-held electric whisk to beat ingredients, for example cream or egg whites.

KNEAD

To handle dough in a strong manner – essential in breadmaking to develop the gluten.

GARNISH

To finish a dish with savoury toppings, usually herbs or spices

PARBOIL

To partially cook an ingredient in boiling water.

PROVE

To allow a homemade dough to rise in a warm area.

BASTE

To spoon cooking juices over food to keep it moist, usually during cooking.

POACH

To simmer slowly in a pan of liquid (often stock or milk).

FOLD

To gently combine ingredients while taking care not to knock out all the air, for example when adding flour to a cake batter.

20 FOOD HACKS

Why not try to make things in the kitchen a little easier?
Try these food hacks for yourself – they really do work!

☐ PLASTIC BOTTLE TO TRANSFER AN EGG YOLK

Finished that plastic bottle? Crack an egg into
a bowl and take a clean, empty plastic bottle.
Squeeze it slightly, hover the top over the yolk
and release the bottle. It will lift the egg yolk
straight out.

☐ RIPEN A BANANA

Place the bananas you'd like ripened in a brown
paper bag, then roll up the bag so it is completely
closed. This traps the ethylene gas that is naturally
emitted by bananas and which encourages
ripening in the bag so the bananas ripen more
quickly.

☐ RIPEN AN AVOCADO

Use the trick above to ripen avocados – just
put them in a brown paper bag with a banana
alongside.

☐ LOOSEN UP BROWN SUGAR

If you microwave brown sugar next to a glass of
water in short bursts, the moisture created from
the water in the microwave will help break down
the brown sugar. Keep your eye on it though!

☐ PIT CHERRIES/HULL STRAWBERRIES WITH EASE

Cherries can be put individually on top of an
empty bottle with the lid removed (they should
fit snugly), then pitted by pushing through a
chopstick. You can also hull a strawberry by
pushing a straw through the middle to hollow
out the centre!

☐ PEEL GINGER WITH A SPOON

Peeling fresh ginger with a knife is just too fiddly
– grab a teaspoon and rub it over the ginger – the
skin literally falls off. I love this hack and use it all
the time.

☐ GET MAXIMUM JUICE FROM CITRUS FRUIT

Keep your citrus fruit in the fridge and then give
it a short blast in the microwave for about
15 seconds. Give the fruit a gentle roll with your
hand on a board to loosen up before juicing.

☐ INSTANT CITRUS WATER

While we're on the citrus front, keep slices of
lemon or lime in the freezer in a sealed bag for a
hot day. Whenever you need some citrus water,
pop one out of the freezer into your glass of water
for an ice-cold citrus kick.

☐ CUT A CAKE WITH PRECISION

A fave of Mrs Barry's – use dental floss to cut a
freshly baked cake like a boss. Portion control
with accuracy!

☐ TOUGH BUTTERNUT SQUASH?

Chuck a butternut squash in the microwave for a couple of minutes to soften it slightly; it'll also make it a breeze to deseed and chop.

☐ STICKY MEASURING PROBLEMS?

Trying to measure out golden syrup or honey can be a real pain. Stick a spoon in hot water to heat briefly or use a little spray of oil so it slides off with ease. This tip has helped me many a time.

☐ OVERBOILING PAN?

Place a wooden spoon across a pan. The water actually avoids the handle of the spoon because wood doesn't conduct heat very well.

☐ REHEAT THAT PIZZA

A bit like the brown sugar hack; put a little glass of water in the microwave with the pizza (or other baked goods) and heat on short bursts to add moisture to the air.

☐ STOP THE CAKE GOING STALE

Seriously, put a slice of bread on a freshly baked cake in the tin if you're not going to eat it immediately. It really does stop the cake going stale.

☐ SLIPPERY CHOPPING BOARD?

Grab a small tea towel, run it under the tap and squeeze it out so that it is just damp. Place it under your cutting board and it'll stop sliding around. I use this in all my videos when using a board.

☐ KEEP KNIVES SHARP (IT'S SAFER THAT WAY)

After you have finished chopping use the back of your knife to transfer food from the board to the pan or bowl – this stops the blade losing sharpness.

☐ CLEAR ICE CUBES

Wanna impress your friends with crystal clear ice cubes you can look straight through? Simply fill your ice-cube trays with boiled water from the kettle.

☐ HERB AND WINE CUBES

Use an ice-cube tray to portion up leftover herbs in melted butter for a ready-made handy flavour punch to add to your pan. This also works with wine; chuck frozen wine cubes in a bolognese or casserole.

☐ PEEL SHALLOTS LIKE A PRO

Niggly things to peel, aren't they? Place them in some boiling water for 8–10 minutes and the skins should just fall off.

☐ BRING MELTED BUTTER BACK TO SOLID

Give your melted butter an ice bath! Place a bowl of melted butter in a larger bowl filled with ice and cold water.

BASIC RECIPES

It's important to have a few basic recipes up your sleeve to get you by. Here are a few of my favourites – you'll use these again and again in your cooking.

BÉCHAMEL SAUCE

A roux is a great way to make sauces with a slightly thicker consistency, for example cheese sauce and gravy. You basically combine equal parts of butter and flour in a pan over a low heat, stirring until they combine to make a loose paste. This also briefly cooks the flour, removing the floury/starchy taste – you then add a liquid to thicken into a sauce. If you melt the butter slightly longer before adding the flour, until it darkens and smells more nutty (usually a couple of minutes), this will create a good base for darker sauces.

MAKES 500ML
50g plain flour
50g butter
550ml milk

1. Melt the butter in a saucepan, then add in the flour and stir until combined. Cook for a couple of minutes to cook the flour. Once you have the thickened roux, pour in half the milk and stir constantly over a low heat; it will be lumpy at first but keep going until it thickens.

2. Gradually add more milk, stirring over a low heat, then switch to a whisk, whisking any lumps. Simmering for a few more minutes over a low heat will give you a nice thickened sauce.

Variations
• Add freshly chopped parsley for a parsley sauce
• Add grated cheese and stir through to melt for a cheese sauce
• Add a combination of Dijon mustard and honey for a honey mustard sauce

MAYONNAISE

I was so surprised when I learned how to make mayonnaise from scratch; it literally takes seconds and is amazingly fresh, plus you can tweak it to your liking and get it tasting exactly how you like. Add things like Tabasco sauce or herbs and spices to start tweaking it further.

MAKES 200ML
1 large egg yolk
210ml olive oil
½ garlic clove
1 tsp lemon juice
1 heaped tsp English mustard
salt and pepper

1. Tip the egg yolk into a small food processor and whizz briefly, then drizzle in the oil in small amounts, pulsing it as you go, until the egg yolk and oil are fully emulsified.

2. Tip in the garlic clove, lemon juice and mustard and whizz until combined and the garlic has been completely chopped through the mixture. Season to taste with salt and pepper.

PESTO

Pesto is easy to get hold of in the shops, but also very simple and even better homemade. All you need is a blender if you want to be super-lazy, or you could use a pestle and mortar.

MAKES 300ML
100g pine nuts, toasted
100g grated Parmesan
large handful of fresh basil
zest of ½ lemon
200ml olive oil
salt and pepper

1. Whizz the pine nuts, Parmesan, basil and lemon zest together in a food processor and then add the oil. It's best to add the oil gradually so you can tweak the texture slightly – if you want it thicker add a little less oil.

2. Season to taste. This will keep for a couple of weeks in an airtight container in the fridge.

VEGETABLE STOCK

Homemade stocks are so easy to make and can be portioned up and stored in the freezer until needed.

MAKES 750ML
1 tbsp olive oil
1 onion, peeled and diced
1 celery stick, diced (add the leaves, too)
1 carrot, diced
4 garlic cloves, peeled and chopped
3 spring onions, chopped
handful of fresh parsley
few sprigs of thyme
1 bay leaf
salt and pepper

1. Heat the oil in a large pan over a low–medium heat, add all the vegetables and herbs and cook gently for 10 minutes to soften.

2. Pour in 1 litre of water and season with salt and pepper. Bring to the boil and then simmer for 40 minutes.

Carefully strain the stock and discard the vegetables and herbs to leave you with a lovely vegetable stock.

CHICKEN STOCK

When you've roasted a chicken for Sunday lunch, don't throw away the carcass – turn it into stock!

MAKES 1.5 LITRES
1 chicken carcass (broken up)
1 onion, peeled and roughly chopped
1 celery stick, roughly chopped
1 carrot, chopped
handful of fresh parsley
1 bay leaf
salt and pepper

1. Put all of the ingredients into a large pan, cover with 2 litres of water and bring to a fast boil. Reduce the heat, cover with a lid and leave to simmer over a low heat for 1½ hours, skimming any fat from the surface every so often.

2. Strain the stock and discard the carcass and vegetables. Allow to cool before storing in the fridge or freezer.

SHORTCRUST PASTRY

I often use ready-made pastry when I'm pressed for time but making your own is actually pretty easy. The trick is to keep your hands nice and cool and to use really cold water to bind the pastry together.

225g plain flour
pinch of salt
112g chilled butter, cut into cubes
cold water

1. Sift the flour and salt into a large bowl, giving a gentle stir to combine. Add the butter and use your fingers and thumbs to rub the butter into the flour – keep going until the mixture resembles breadcrumbs.

2. Gradually add cold water, a tablespoon at a time, until the mixture comes together nicely. Don't add too much water – you just need enough to bring the pastry together in the bowl (use a fork to stir it in).

3. Wrap the pastry in cling film and chill in the fridge for about 20 minutes before rolling out on a floured surface.

This chapter is a gentle introduction to the book, easing you in with recipes that make you, well . . . feel good. Of course, there are slightly healthier ones too, such as the Sweet Potato & Kale Hash or the Salmon Rosti Islands, but for me the phrase 'feel-good' can be something else: a dish that makes you proud of your achievement in some way. For me this could be something like the Steak & Roast New Potato Salad or slightly naughty Squidgy Beetroot Brownies. It's all about balance. Each of the recipes in this chapter uses some really interesting combinations, making use of ingredients and food trends that have cropped up in recent years and, of course, everything I've learned to date.

Some of my personal favourites in this chapter are the Caprese Chicken Salad, thanks to its gorgeous taste, eye-catching colour and simplicity and the Coconut Crumbed Chicken, which just works an absolute charm – I'm super-proud of that one. And for a real feel-good, cosy dish it has to be the Chicken, Porcini & Barley Soup – a super-chunky, hearty dish that is perfect for a winter night.

Give the recipes a go and don't forget to reach out on social media to let me know the recipes that make you feel good too!

1.
FEEL-GOOD RECIPES

CHICKEN, PORCINI & BARLEY SOUP

Hearty, warming and filling sums up this soup brilliantly – it's fab on a cold night to warm the cockles. It's very chunky – almost like a stew – with a slight woody vibe from the porcini, although you can reserve a little chicken stock to thin it out just before serving, if you prefer. The barley adds a fantastic texture along with the poached chicken, plus you can make and serve up this gorgeous, hassle-free soup in just one pan.

READY IN 50 MINUTES
SERVES 4

25g porcini
1 tsp butter
1 onion, peeled and diced
1 large carrot, peeled and chopped
    into small chunks
2 celery sticks, sliced into small
    chunks
120g pearl barley
400g chicken breasts, cut into
    small chunks
500ml chicken stock
1 bay leaf
handful of spinach, torn
handful of chopped flat-leaf parsley,
    plus extra for sprinkling
salt and pepper

1. Start by putting the porcini into a bowl and pouring over 250ml boiling water. Leave to one side for 25 minutes to soften, then remove the porcini, drain on kitchen paper and slice roughly. Strain the porcini soaking liquid through a sieve a couple of times (to remove any grit). Reserve to use later in the soup.

2. When the porcini have about 15 minutes left to soak, melt the butter in a large saucepan over a medium heat. Add the onion, carrot and celery and season well with salt and pepper. Cook the vegetables, stirring well, until the onions just start to brown at the edges, about 10 minutes.

3. Next tip in the barley and chicken chunks, stirring to coat in the butter, and let them cook for a couple of minutes. Add the chicken stock, bay leaf and the porcini and their liquid, then top with 350ml water. Stir well and bring to a simmer.

4. Put a lid on the saucepan and simmer for 25 minutes until the liquid has reduced down and the barley is nice and puffed up. Add the spinach and parsley for the final 5 minutes of cooking. Remove the bay leaf and taste and adjust the seasoning. Serve in bowls with a fresh sprinkle of parsley – it's great with some buttered baguette slices.

♟ **VIRGIN TIP**
During the simmering remove the lid a couple of times and stir the bottom of the pan; sometimes some of the barley can settle there so keep it moving. You can also top up with more water if you like a thinner soup – I'm just a fan of it being chunky.

COCONUT CRUMBED CHICKEN WITH WARM MIXED BEAN SALAD

I absolutely love this recipe. It's a perfect combo of customisable warmed bean salad and gorgeous mango and coconut coated chicken breasts. The chicken strips also work well on their own, served with some extra mango chutney as a dip.

READY IN 30 MINUTES
SERVES 4

olive oil, for drizzling
600g chicken breasts, cut into finger-
    width slices
2 tbsp mango chutney
6 tbsp breadcrumbs
2 tbsp desiccated coconut
salt and pepper

FOR THE SALAD

500g mixed beans of your choice –
    try sliced runner beans, tinned
    cannellini beans, frozen soya beans
    or tinned butter beans
large handful of tinned or frozen
    sweetcorn, drained or defrosted
3 spring onions, thinly sliced
2 celery sticks, thinly sliced
handful of flat-leaf parsley, chopped
handful of coriander, chopped
1 tbsp Dijon mustard
1 tbsp balsamic vinegar
2 tbsp maple syrup
1 tbsp olive oil

1. Preheat the oven to 200°C/180°C fan/400°F/Gas mark 6 and drizzle a little oil over the bottom of an oven tray.

2. Put the chicken pieces into a bowl with the mango chutney and toss until all the chicken is well coated. Put the breadcrumbs and coconut in a sealable food bag, season with salt and pepper, then add the chicken pieces and shake the bag well so that each piece of chicken has a covering. Tip the chicken into the oven tray and bake in the hot oven for 10–12 minutes, turning once.

3. Meanwhile make the bean salad. If you are using fresh beans, slice and cook in a large saucepan of boiling water for 5–7 minutes, or until they're tender. Add any frozen beans and the sweetcorn to the boiling water then drain any tinned beans and add those too. Stir and heat for 1–2 minutes. Drain the beans well and return to the pan. Stir through the spring onions, celery and herbs.

4. In a separate bowl combine the mustard, vinegar, maple syrup and olive oil. Pour over the beans and toss well.

5. Once the chicken is cooked serve with the warm bean salad.

🍴 **VIRGIN TIP**
You can freeze the chicken once it has been coated in the breadcrumb and coconut mixture, as long as you are not using chicken that has previously been frozen. When you're ready to cook, preheat the oven and roast the chicken from frozen as above, increasing the cooking time to 20 minutes.

CAPRESE CHICKEN SALAD

A super-speedy, refreshing chicken salad inspired by the traditional 'Caprese' combination of tomatoes, basil and mozzarella. Here I've added baked pesto chicken and a drizzle of balsamic for a deliciously light, yet filling salad.

READY IN 30 MINUTES
SERVES 4

butter, for greasing
400g mini chicken fillets
3 tbsp pesto
300g cherry tomatoes (a mix of yellow and red cherry tomatoes works really well)
2 x 125g mozzarella balls
small bunch of basil leaves
olive oil, for drizzling
balsamic vinegar, for drizzling to taste
salt and pepper

1. Preheat the oven to 180°C/160°C fan/350°F/Gas mark 4 and lightly grease a baking dish with some butter.

2. Put the mini chicken fillets into the dish, add the pesto and use a spatula to push the fillets around until they are all coated with pesto. Bake in the oven for 25 minutes, or until fully cooked through. Transfer to a chopping board and leave to cool for a few minutes before slicing into chunks.

3. Meanwhile cut the tomatoes into quarters, removing the seeds if you wish, and tip into a large bowl. Cut or tear your mozzarella into small chunks, tear the basil leaves into smaller pieces and add both to the bowl too. Drizzle over some olive oil, season with salt and pepper and and stir well to combine.

4. Tip the salad into a serving dish and put the chicken pieces on top. Finish with a drizzle of balsamic vinegar and serve.

♟ **VIRGIN TIP**
Mini fillets are used here for the shorter baking time – you can use chicken breasts or thighs but you'll need to increase the baking time to make sure they're cooked through.

TERIYAKI PORK LOIN & EGG-FRIED RICE

This is a tantalisingly tasty – yet simple – recipe. Delicious pork tenderloin is baked and drenched in a teriyaki glaze and served with some good old egg-fried rice. This really is a perfect combination of simplicity and cheeky flavour.

READY IN 50 MINUTES
SERVES 4

60ml mirin
3 tbsp soy sauce
3 tbsp caster sugar
1 garlic clove, peeled and crushed
2cm piece of fresh ginger, peeled
    and grated
600g pork tenderloin

FOR THE RICE
1 large egg
1 tbsp soy sauce
2 tsp sesame oil
2 pak choy, sliced lengthways
2 spring onions, sliced
500g cooked rice

♟ VIRGIN TIP
Check the pork is cooked through by cutting into the thickest part and making sure there's no pink remaining.

1. Preheat the oven to 200°C/180°C fan/400°F/Gas mark 6.

2. Put the mirin, soy, sugar, garlic and ginger into a small saucepan. Bring to a simmer over a medium heat and cook until thickened and sauce-like, about 5 minutes.

3. Put the pork tenderloin into an oven dish that will hold it snugly and drizzle the sauce over the top and down the sides. Cook in the oven for 40 minutes, basting two or three times during cooking.

4. While the pork is cooking, prepare the rice. Beat the egg and 1 teaspoon of the soy sauce together. Heat half the sesame oil in a wok and scramble the egg until just cooked. Remove from the pan and put to one side. Heat the remaining oil in the wok over medium-high heat and stir-fry the pak choy for 3–4 minutes until it starts to brown but retains some crispness. Tip the spring onions and rice into the pan, toss and stir then return the egg to the pan. Toss everything together with the remaining soy sauce.

5. Once the pork is cooked, remove from the oven and cut into thick slices. Serve with the egg-fried rice, drizzled with the sauce from the pan.

CHORIZO & SPINACH SCRAMBLED EGG BAGELS

A delicious mouthful of tangy chorizo alongside spring-oniony scrambled eggs and spinach is a great way to start the day. The ingredients are minimal and it's all made in a flash, so it's a really good filler to get you going in the morning, but also works well for lunch or in the evening. A proper no-hassle recipe.

READY IN 10 MINUTES
SERVES 4

8 eggs
splash of milk
4 spring onions, sliced
4 bagels
200g cooking chorizo, diced
knob of butter, plus extra for
    spreading
4 large handfuls of baby spinach
salt and pepper

1. Beat the eggs and milk together in a bowl, season with salt and pepper then stir in the spring onions.

2. Preheat the grill while you slice the bagels in half. Put the bagels under the grill and toast the cut side.

3. Meanwhile, place a frying pan over a medium-high heat and cook the chorizo until it's browned and crisp. Turn off the heat and tip away the excess fat but keep the chorizo in the pan.

4. Melt the butter in a saucepan over a low-medium heat, tip in the eggs and stir. While the eggs are scrambling, put the spinach in with the warm chorizo, return to a medium heat and toss. Let the spinach wilt while you butter the bagels and stir the scrambled eggs. The eggs should be only just set.

5. Put the buttered bagels on plates, top with the chorizo and spinach then spoon the scrambled eggs on top.

🎩 VIRGIN TIP
This meal is super-quick but everything happens at once so you need to be organised and have everything laid out ready at the start. Keep an eye on the bagels as you do not want them to burn (you could also toast them in your toaster).

LAMB KEBABS WITH SESAME FLATBREAD

I love the ease of this recipe; I think that's what makes me feel good about it. That pleasing comfort of knowing that you've got a sneaky recipe up your sleeve to rely on. Marinated lamb with a quick fix accompaniment alongside (a sort of food hack really) using ready made flatbreads/chapatti but just taking them up a notch with mustard and sesame seeds – winner!

**READY IN 30 MINUTES,
PLUS MARINATING TIME
SERVES 4**

90ml tikka masala curry paste
300ml natural yoghurt
1 lime, zested
6–8 sprigs of coriander, leaves and
    stalks roughly chopped
700g lamb leg, cut into bite-size
    chunks
mixed salad leaves, to serve

FOR THE BREAD
2 tsp black mustard seeds
2 tsp sesame seeds
40g butter
8 paratha, chapatti or flatbreads

1. Mix together the curry paste, yoghurt, lime zest (save the lime for squeezing later) and the coriander. Add the lamb pieces to the bowl and stir so everything is coated. Cover with cling film and leave in the fridge to marinate for at least 2 hours or overnight.

2. When you are ready to cook, prepare the butter for the flatbreads. Heat the black mustard and sesame seeds in a small dry frying pan over a medium heat. When they pop and become fragrant remove from the heat and add the butter to the pan. Allow it to melt and combine with the seeds.

3. Thread the marinated lamb on to 8 skewers while you preheat a griddle pan or grill – or even a barbecue. Cook for 2–3 minutes on all sides until they are browned on the outside and slightly pink in the centre.

4. While the kebabs are cooking, put a large frying pan over a low heat and warm the flatbreads through, one at a time. Once each is warmed, brush with the seedy butter and keep warm in a low oven.

5. Serve the kebabs and flatbreads with the salad leaves and a squeeze of lime juice.

♙ VIRGIN TIP
If you are using wooden skewers soak them in water for about 30 minutes before using; if you forget, wrap a little foil around the exposed skewer to prevent it burning.

LAMB & GINGER
POTSTICKER DUMPLINGS

I've tried dumplings a couple of times in my life, but only in various Asian restaurants over here – obviously the dream has to be to head out to Asia and try some in situ. The last dumplings I had were a delicious lamb and ginger combination that I've replicated here as a starter with a little tweaked plum sauce. I think you'll love them – enjoy!

READY IN 25 MINUTES
SERVES 4

150g lamb mince
2 tbsp soy sauce
1 tsp sesame oil, plus extra for frying
2cm piece of fresh ginger, peeled and
    finely grated
1 garlic clove, peeled and finely grated
1 small carrot, peeled and finely grated
4 spring onions, thinly sliced
small bunch of coriander, chopped
16 ready-made dumpling wrappers

FOR THE DIPPING SAUCE
3 tbsp Chinese plum sauce from a jar
2 tsp sesame oil
1 tsp soy sauce
pinch of chilli flakes

1. Put all the ingredients, except the dumpling wrappers, into a large bowl and mix well.

2. To fill the dumplings, take a dumpling wrapper in your hand and spoon a heaped teaspoon of the lamb into the centre. Wet around the edges a little and fold in half to create a semicircle, then press the edges to seal so it looks like a little Cornish pasty. Repeat with the remaining wrappers and filling.

3. Bring a large saucepan of water to the boil and gently slide in the dumplings. Stir the water until the pan comes back to the boil and cook until the dumplings rise to the surface and the water is at a rolling boil. Cook for a further minute then remove with a slotted spoon.

4. Heat a little extra oil in a frying pan over a medium-high heat. Once hot sit the dumplings in the pan to brown their bottoms for 3–5 minutes. Once brown and slightly crisped, remove from the pan, drain on kitchen paper and put on a serving plate.

5. The dipping sauce it simply a pimped-up version of shop-bought plum sauce. Combine the jarred sauce with the remaining ingredients, stir well and taste, adding more chilli if you like. Serve the warm dumplings with a bowl of sauce. Stonking!

🎩 **VIRGIN TIP**
Mix up the fillings with other vegetables and meats such as pork or chicken. As with a lot of the recipes in this book, I want to encourage you to get creative and put your twist on things – just don't forget to send me a picture!

BEEF SATAY WITH NASI GORENG

Satay is up there for me flavour-wise; it's an excuse to have peanut butter in a recipe, but as I'm sure you are aware it's a classic combo. This recipe, although not the lightest in this chapter, makes me feel good – it's full of flavour. The nasi goreng rice is pushing the boat out a little but it really is worth the effort and it's a great way to get you experimenting in the kitchen!

3 tbsp Thai red curry paste
4 tbsp crunchy peanut butter
250ml coconut milk
1 tbsp soy sauce
¼–1 tsp chilli flakes (optional)
2 tsp sugar
600g rump steak, trimmed and sliced
   into strips

FOR THE RICE

½ tsp dried shrimp paste
1 tsp sugar
2 garlic cloves, peeled and crushed
1 red chilli, deseeded and finely diced
2cm piece of fresh ginger, peeled
   and grated
1 tbsp tomato purée
1 tbsp soy sauce
2 tbsp groundnut oil
6 large shallots, peeled and thinly
   sliced
2 eggs, beaten with a drop of water
1 red pepper, deseeded and cut into
   small chunks
250g cooked long-grain rice
1 tbsp light soy sauce
4 spring onions, chopped
1 tbsp chopped unsalted peanuts
1 lime, cut into wedges

👨‍🍳 VIRGIN TIP

Dried shrimp paste is available in
most supermarkets now – look in
the 'speciality ingredients' or 'world
foods' aisle. However if you don't
have any you can use fish
sauce instead.

1. Start by making the satay sauce. Cook the curry paste in a saucepan over a medium heat for 1 minute until it becomes fragrant. Stir in the peanut butter, coconut milk, soy sauce, chilli (if using) and sugar. Warm through and stir until well combined. Put the sauce to one side to cool completely.

2. Drizzle about one-third of the satay sauce over the meat, cover and marinate in the fridge for at least 3 hours, or overnight.

3. Now start on the rice. Put the shrimp paste and sugar in a bowl with a tablespoon of boiling water and stir until the sugar dissolves and you have a smooth paste. Stir in the garlic, chilli, ginger, tomato purée and soy sauce so everything is well combined.

4. Heat 1½ tablespoons of the oil in a large frying pan or wok and fry the shallots over a medium heat until they are crisp and brown. Fish them out with a slotted spoon and drain on kitchen paper. If the pan is dry add the remaining sesame oil, then pour in the beaten eggs and scramble them; remove from the pan once cooked.

5. Preheat the grill or a griddle pan to high while you thread the steak on to 12 skewers (see tip on page 29). Cook for 4–5 minutes on each side until cooked through.

6. Meanwhile gently reheat the remaining satay sauce in a small saucepan and turn up the heat under the wok. Cook the paste in the wok for 1 minute to release the spices, then add the pepper and fry for 2–3 minutes. Add the rice, stirring and cooking until everything is heated through and amalgamated (add a drop of oil if it starts to stick). Return the egg to the pan along with the soy sauce and fork through.

7. Divide the rice between four plates and top with three skewers per plate. Sprinkle over the crispy shallots, spring onions and peanuts. Give everything a squeeze of lime and serve with the extra satay sauce for dipping.

STEAK & ROAST NEW POTATO SALAD

A delightful combo of sesame-infused roasted new potatoes, with strips of steak in a speedy dressing, this is just what the doctor ordered: deliciously light but enough to fill you up and satisfy your hunger craving.

READY IN 50 MINUTES
SERVES 4

400g Jersey royal new potatoes
2 tbsp sesame oil, plus extra
    for rubbing
600g sirloin steak
salt and pepper

FOR THE DRESSING
2 tbsp sesame oil
2 tbsp white wine vinegar
2 tbsp orange juice
2 tbsp runny honey
1 tsp sesame seeds

TO SERVE
150g beansprouts, washed
250g mixed salad leaves, washed
2 tbsp chopped coriander

1. Preheat the oven to 190°C/170°C fan/375°F/Gas mark 5.

2. Bring a large saucepan of water to the boil and parboil the new potatoes for 20 minutes. Drain and tip into a baking tray. Pour the sesame oil into the tray and mix with a spatula to coat the potatoes, then season with salt and pepper and mix again lightly to coat all over. Bake in the hot oven for 25 minutes, or until golden brown. Remove and put to one side to cool.

3. While the potatoes are in the oven, rub the steak with a little sesame oil and season with salt and pepper. Place a frying pan over a high heat and when hot, add the steak. Sear for 3 minutes on each side (increase the cooking time if you like your steak well done). Remove from the pan and rest on a board for 10 minutes before slicing into strips.

4. Mix all the dressing ingredients together in a bowl and leave to one side.

5. To serve, put the salad leaves into a serving bowl and scatter over the beansprouts and coriander. Add the roasted potatoes and tuck the steak strips in between. Give the whole lot a generous dousing of dressing and enjoy.

♟ VIRGIN TIP
This salad and dressing combo works brilliantly with other meats – grilled chicken is a lovely alternative but the steak is Mrs Barry's favourite.

COD NUGGETS WITH KATSU DIP

Forget chicken nuggets – let's try and give cod nuggets some love! These are a fantastic light treat but can easily be taken up a notch by serving with some rice or couscous for a family meal. Make the sauce ahead and keep in a sealed container in the fridge so it's ready when you decide to make your nuggets. You can then dunk away to your heart's content in the gorgeous katsu dip.

READY IN 35 MINUTES
SERVES 4

1 tsp oil
400g chunky cod fillet, cut into
    bite-size cubes
1 egg, beaten
90g panko breadcrumbs
lime wedges, to serve

FOR THE DIP

2 tsp sesame oil
1 small onion, peeled and finely diced
1 garlic clove, peeled and crushed
4cm piece of fresh ginger, peeled
    and grated
2 tsp curry powder
1 tsp turmeric
1 tbsp plain flour
350ml vegetable stock
1 tbsp honey
1 tbsp soy sauce
40g creamed coconut

1. Start with the dip. Heat the oil in a saucepan over a low heat, add the diced onion, cover and cook gently for 10 minutes until soft. Add the garlic and ginger and stir for a minute. Stir in the curry powder, turmeric and flour, cook for a minute, then slowly pour in the stock, stirring all the time, until it comes to a simmer. Stir in the honey, soy sauce and creamed coconut and put to one side while you make the nuggets.

2. Preheat the oven to 200°C/180°C fan/400°F/Gas mark 6 and grease a non-stick baking tray with the oil.

3. Line up everything you need on the work surface: a plate with the fish pieces, a shallow bowl of beaten egg and a plate spread with the breadcrumbs. Dip a piece of fish into the egg so it's covered, then put into the breadcrumbs, toss until fully coated and put on the baking tray. Repeat with all the fish and then bake in the hot oven for 10 minutes until it is cooked through.

4. When the cod is done reheat the sauce. Serve the cod nuggets with lime wedges to squeeze over and the katsu dip for dipping.

🎩 **VIRGIN TIP**
If you don't finish the sauce, it's great with a bag of chip shop chips! You can use frozen cod fillets for this recipe; just defrost thoroughly and pat dry with kitchen paper before using.

SRIRACHA PRAWNS WITH GIANT COUSCOUS

I find this such a refreshing recipe: it's got a little bit of a kick, but you can easily control the heat levels. Here we're cooking prawns in a little sriracha hot sauce and serving them with a pile of giant couscous salad and caramelised red onion.

READY IN 25 MINUTES
SERVES 4

350g raw prawns, peeled and veins
    removed
3 tbsp chopped flat-leaf parsley
juice of 1 orange
2 garlic cloves, peeled and crushed
½ tsp dried chilli flakes
2–3 tsp sriracha sauce (or to taste)
1 vegetable stock cube
180g giant couscous
1 tbsp olive oil
1 small red onion, peeled and thinly
    sliced
3 tomatoes, halved, seeds removed
    and diced
½ cucumber, halved lengthways, seeds
    removed and diced
salt and pepper

1. Put the prawns into a bowl and add 1 tablespoon of the parsley, half the orange juice, the garlic, the dried chilli flakes and 1 teaspoon of the sriracha sauce and mix around to coat fully. If you're not cooking the prawns immediately, cover the bowl with cling film and chill in the fridge.

2. Bring a saucepan of water to the boil and crumble in the stock cube, stirring to dissolve. Add the couscous and cook according to the packet instructions. Drain and allow to cool, then tip into a bowl.

3. Meanwhile heat the olive oil in a frying pan over a medium heat and add the onion. Cook for 10 minutes until it softens and starts to caramelise, stirring in a dash of sriracha sauce for the last 30 seconds. Tip the onion into the bowl of couscous and return the frying pan to the heat. Add the prawns and marinade to the frying pan and cook for 5 minutes, stirring regularly, until the prawns turn pink and tender.

4. Meanwhile add the tomato and cucumber to the couscous long with another tablespoon of parsley. Squeeze in the juice from the other half of the orange, and mix well. Give it all a good season with salt and pepper then, if you like, add another dash of sriracha for extra kick.

5. Serve a pile of the couscous with a good heap of the prawns on top, the remaining parsley sprinkled over the prawns and a final squeeze of the orange half.

🍳 **VIRGIN TIP**
Mrs Barry is not a huge fan of sriracha, so I keep this mild when making it for her, omitting it from the onion step. It's all about tweaking it to your liking – the recipe allows for a great deal of flexibility so keep an extra bit of orange and the sriracha handy when serving up.

SALMON RÖSTI ISLANDS WITH LEMON HORSERADISH

It looks pretty fancy but this lovely, light, refreshing bite is a doddle to make. A potato rösti island smothered in a lemon horseradish sauce with dill and salmon strips on top – a real feel-good recipe.

READY IN 20 MINUTES
SERVES 4

200g Greek yoghurt
1 tbsp horseradish sauce
zest and juice of ½ lemon
500g waxy potatoes, peeled
    and grated
1 egg, beaten
2 tbsp plain flour
knob of butter, melted
olive oil, for frying
1 x 120g packet of smoked salmon,
    cut into strips
handful of fresh dill
salt and pepper

1. Make the horseradish sauce first so it can chill in the fridge. In a bowl combine the yoghurt, horseradish, lemon zest and juice plus a good pinch of salt and a grinding of pepper in a bowl. Mix until combined, taste and tweak until you're happy, then keep in the fridge until you need it.

2. Now for the potatoes: push the grated potato through a colander to squeeze out as much liquid as you can. Tip from the colander on to sheets of kitchen paper and pat dry, then put into a bowl. Add the egg, flour and butter and stir well to completely coat. Season with salt and pepper.

3. Put some olive oil into a frying pan and warm over a medium heat. Using clean hands, shape some potato mixture into a typical burger-sized patty shape – you want to make them quite thin as they are not as delicate as you think. Put two or three into the pan and flatten slightly with a spatula to spread out. Cook for a couple of minutes until golden brown, then flip over and cook the other side. Remove and drain on kitchen paper while you repeat with the rest of the mixture, topping up the oil in the pan as needed.

4. Serve the rösti on a plate with a good dollop of the horseradish sauce on top, a strip of smoked salmon, a little grinding of black pepper and a few dill sprigs. Delicious.

♟ VIRGIN TIP
It's important to keep the rösti thin, otherwise the middle will still contain bits of uncooked potato.

SWEET POTATO & KALE HASH

I like recipes that provide maximum taste with minimum effort and this dish is that in a nutshell. It uses superfood sweet potato and turns it into a light hash with kale, shallots and cumin, all rounded off with a little hot sauce (add as much or as little as you like). I really think you'll love this dish, especially when topped with a fried egg.

READY IN 20 MINUTES
MAKES 4

2 large sweet potatoes, peeled and cut
    into small chunks
3 tbsp olive oil
2 shallots, peeled and thinly sliced
4 handfuls of sweetcorn (frozen is fine)
2 tsp garlic granules
2 tsp cumin seeds
4 large handfuls of shredded kale, any
    thick stalks removed
4 eggs (optional)
2 avocados, sliced
1 lime, cut into wedges
1–2 dashes of hot sauce (optional)
salt and pepper

1. Fill a saucepan with water from a just-boiled kettle, add the sweet potato chunks and bring back to the boil. Simmer gently for around 7 minutes until softened, then drain and leave to steam dry.

2. Heat 2 tablespoons of the oil in a large frying pan over a medium heat. Tip the sweet potatoes into the hot pan with the shallots, sweetcorn, garlic granules, cumin seeds and kale. Toss to coat in the oil and season with salt and pepper. Cook, stirring occasionally, until the veg is browned and toasty, about 10–15 minutes.

3. If you want to serve the hash with fried eggs, while the veg is cooking heat the remaining oil in another non-stick frying pan and fry the eggs until done the way you like them.

4. Tip the vegetables into four bowls and top each with a fried egg and some sliced avocado. Serve with lime wedges to squeeze over and a few dashes of hot sauce.

🎩 **VIRGIN TIP**
You can pad this out further by adding other vegetables – try some grated raw carrot for a different texture.

SESAME HALLOUMI BITES WITH SWEET PEPPER SAUCE

Halloumi is such a versatile cheese and works with lots of different flavours. In this recipe cubes are coated in a layer of golden sesame seeds and fried, then served with a mild sweet pepper dip. A perfect starter – although you could also serve as a party snack.

READY IN 20 MINUTES
SERVES 4

100g sesame seeds
1 egg, beaten
25g plain flour
250g block halloumi cheese, cut
    into about 16 small squares
vegetable oil, for frying
pepper

FOR THE SWEET PEPPER SAUCE

1 large red pepper, deseeded and
    roughly chopped
3 garlic cloves, peeled
100g caster sugar
50ml distilled malt vinegar
1 tbsp cornflour, mixed to a paste
    with 2½ tbsp water

♟ VIRGIN TIP
The sweet pepper sauce is mild but tangy. To add more kick to the sauce chuck in a red chilli (including the seeds) when whizzing the mixture together.

1. Start with the sweet pepper sauce. Put the red pepper, garlic, sugar and vinegar into a mini food processor with 180ml water. Whizz for 30 seconds or so to combine fully; it should look like a thin chilli sauce and the sugar should be fully dissolved.

2. Pour this mixture into a small saucepan, place over a low heat and bring to a simmer (this won't take long due to the sugar content). Add the cornflour paste and stir through over a low simmer. After a few minutes, it should be noticeably thicker. Remove from the heat, pour into a jar to cool and set aside.

3. Put the sesame seeds, beaten egg and flour into separate, shallow bowls. Season the flour with a little freshly ground black pepper. Take a cube of halloumi and roll in the flour to coat, then dunk in the beaten egg. Next roll the egg-coated cube in the sesame seeds to fully coat it. You can always dunk again if you want a better coating. Repeat this step with the other cheese cubes and leave them to one side. Use one hand for the whole process – makes it a lot cleaner!

4. Pour enough vegetable oil into a small saucepan to come at least a third of the way up the sides and place over a medium-high heat. You want it hot enough that a small piece of bread sizzles when placed in the oil, but not so hot that it browns the cubes too quickly, so adjust the temperature as you go. Fry in small batches until golden brown, resting on kitchen paper as you remove them carefully from the oil.

5. Serve with cocktail sticks so you can dunk the bites in the sweet pepper dip.

COURGETTI WITH RED PEPPER & SUNFLOWER SEED PESTO

This is a delightfully simple recipe packed with flavour. Spiralising is a really clever way of boosting your daily veg count. Making courgetti and serving it with the yummy red pepper pesto will really rock your socks. It's refreshing and light, but still filling and is a personal favourite of Mrs Barry's. The bacon lardons are optional and could be switched up with more greens such as charred courgettes to make it vegetarian. Play with this and experiment with other ingredients and pesto combinations.

READY IN 15 MINUTES
SERVES 4

200g broccoli, cut into bite-size florets
200g smoked lardons
4 courgettes, spiralised or ribboned
    with a peeler

FOR THE PESTO
4 red peppers
4 garlic cloves, unpeeled
1 tbsp olive oil, plus extra for drizzling
85g sunflower seeds
50g Parmesan, grated
1 tsp cayenne pepper
salt

👨‍🍳 **VIRGIN TIP**
The pesto can work really well as a dip – if you have any left over try it with some toasted pitta bread!

1. Start by roasting the peppers for the pesto. Preheat the oven to 200°C/180°C fan/400°F/Gas mark 6.

2. Cut the cheeks from the peppers and discard the stems and seeds. Put into a large roasting tin with the garlic, toss with a tablespoon of olive oil and sprinkle with a little salt. Roast for 35 minutes, shaking the pan halfway through to shuffle the veg.

3. While the peppers are cooking, toast the sunflower seeds in a dry frying pan until they start to pop, then put to one side.

4. Remove the peppers and garlic from the oven and squeeze the garlic cloves into a food processor, discarding the skins. Add the roasted peppers, sunflower seeds, Parmesan and cayenne pepper. Whizz until smooth then, with the motor still running, drizzle in some more olive oil until it reaches a pesto consistency.

5. Bring a saucepan of water to the boil and blanch the broccoli for 2 minutes, then drain. Place a large frying pan over a medium heat and cook the lardons until they are browned and crisp. Add the drained broccoli to the pan, toss in the bacon fat and let it cook and char for a few minutes. Throw in the courgetti and toss for 1 minute until it starts softening. Spoon over 4–5 tablespoons of the pesto and toss so it evenly coats the veg. Divide into four bowls to serve – gorgeous.

SPICED LENTIL & CHICKPEAS WITH POACHED EGGS

This is a lovely light bite with a slight curry vibe. The combination of spiced chickpeas and lentils with a poached egg plonked on top works brilliantly. The dressing gives it a little edge of lime and Tabasco; you can really play around with the dressing here but an extra squeeze of lime before serving works a charm.

READY IN 40 MINUTES
SERVES 4

180g red lentils
2 tbsp olive oil
2 x 400g tins chickpeas, rinsed and
    drained
4 spring onions, chopped
2 tsp mild curry powder
handful of coriander, plus extra
    to serve
salt and pepper

FOR THE DRESSING
zest and juice of 1 lime
10 drops of Tabasco (or to taste)
pinch of caster sugar
3 tbsp extra-virgin olive oil

TO SERVE
4–8 eggs

🍳 **VIRGIN TIP**
Bacon bits can add another
dimension to this dish if you wish;
simply fry a couple of rashers until
really crispy, slice finely once cooled
and add to the mix. I've also served
it straight out of little gem lettuce
leaves for bowls – works really well!

1. Cook the lentils in boiling water for 30 minutes until soft, or according to the packet instructions.

2. Meanwhile heat the olive oil in a frying pan over a medium heat. Add the drained chickpeas and a pinch of salt and cook for a few minutes to warm through. Add the spring onions and continue to cook, keeping your eye on the chickpeas particularly so that they brown evenly all over. Transfer to a large bowl.

3. Mix half the lime zest and juice in a small bowl with the Tabasco, sugar and olive oil. Taste and tweak with more Tabasco, sugar or lime as required and then put to one side.

4. Meanwhile bring a large saucepan of water to a steady simmer, ready for poaching your eggs.

5. When the lentils are done drain thoroughly, and add to the chickpeas along with the curry powder and fresh coriander. Give everything a gentle mix to coat, then season well with salt and pepper. Pour the lime dressing over the chickpea mixture and stir to coat.

6. To poach your eggs, break them one by one into a ramekin (this will make it easier to slip them into the water). Make a swirl in the water using a spoon and quickly tip in the eggs one at a time. Simmer very gently for about 4 minutes until the egg whites are firm. Carefully remove with a slotted spoon and drain on kitchen paper.

7. Pile the lentils and chickpeas on to plates and top with a poached egg (or two). Finish with a little extra lime juice and a few drops of Tabasco. Scatter over some extra coriander before serving.

SQUIDGY BEETROOT BROWNIES

Brownies? Beetroot? What kind of thing is this? Yes, it's a chocolate brownie with beetroot in it, and boy does it work! After baking these you have gorgeous textured brownies that you would never guess had this hidden ingredient had you not read the title. In fact, why not make some and try them out on your friends?

**READY IN 45 MINUTES,
PLUS COOLING TIME
MAKES 16**

250g good-quality plain chocolate
100g unsalted butter, diced
250g vac-packed cooked beetroot
    (NOT the kind in vinegar or this
    will not taste good!)
3 large eggs
250g soft light brown sugar
150g ground almonds
2 tbsp cocoa powder
1 tsp baking powder
1 tsp vanilla extract
icing sugar, for dusting

1. Preheat the oven to 200°C/180°C fan/400°F/Gas mark 6 and grease and line a 23cm square brownie tin with baking parchment.

2. Break up the chocolate and put into a heatproof bowl along with the butter. Set it over a pan of gently simmering water (making sure the bottom of the bowl doesn't touch the water) and gently melt, stirring as you go.

3. Tip the beetroot into a food processor and whizz to a purée, scraping down the sides of the bowl halfway through. Pour in the melted chocolate mixture then add the eggs and whizz again until combined. Scrape down the sides again then add the sugar, ground almonds, cocoa, baking powder and vanilla and process to a smooth batter.

4. Pour into the prepared tin and bake for 25–30 minutes until the top is set and the middle is still a little soft. Remove from the oven and allow to cool in the tin. Once cool, lift the brownie from the tin and cut into 16 squares. Dust the tops with a little icing sugar.

♟ VIRGIN TIP
If you like a bit of a kick, add a pinch or two of dried chilli flakes when you dust with icing sugar – or even add to the mixture itself!

STEAMED FRUIT WITH VANILLA CREAM

I love this recipe: the combination of the fruit, juices and spices mingled together with a simple vanilla cream is perfect in the warmer months and makes a refreshing dessert. If you have fruit you need to use up you can cook and freeze it in advance and then make the vanilla cream when you're ready to serve. Try making this with pears, rhubarb or peaches too.

READY IN 35 MINUTES
SERVES 4

2 nectarines
4 apricots
4 plums
1 tbsp honey
1 vanilla pod
1 star anise
1 bay leaf
1 cinnamon stick
300ml crème fraîche

1. Preheat the oven to 180°C/160°C fan/350°F/Gas mark 4.

2. Remove the stones from the fruit and cut into halves or quarters depending on their size – you want them all to be roughly the same size. Put them into an oven dish, making sure it's a fairly snug fit, and drizzle with the honey.

3. Scrape the seeds from the vanilla pod and put them aside for later. Put the pod, star anise, bay leaf and cinnamon stick in with the fruit and cover the dish tightly with foil.

4. Cook in the oven for 30 minutes, basting with the spiced juices halfway through (add a splash of water if the dish looks too dry). Meanwhile, beat the vanilla seeds into the crème fraîche.

5. Once cooked, discard the whole spices and divide the cooked fruit and juices into four bowls. Serve with the vanilla cream.

🍳 VIRGIN TIP
Make sure the fruit is really ripe otherwise this will be sour. If it needs a little help in that department, add some extra honey or a sprinkling of vanilla sugar.

A massive part of writing *My Virgin Kitchen* has been about getting kids into the kitchen. My elder daughter Phoebe could crack eggs at 18 months as she's always been involved from a young age. Cooking has brought my family together, and is a fantastic way of making memories with them, letting them be creative and teaching them about food, not to mention having good fun along the way. The recipes in this chapter are either ones that kids can attempt themselves (with a watchful adult eye), or ones to get them eating foods they may not always be keen on, plus a good handful of recipes to get the family round the table eating together.

Oh and if your kid/big kid does make a mess in the kitchen, embrace it; that's what we do in our videos. Far too often cooking is portrayed as being squeaky clean, but I say let the kitchen be a playground – a little flour on the head never hurt anyone!

Favourites in this chapter include the tongue-tingling Pulled Pork Ragu, guaranteed to get the family round the table, the Kids' Pizza Parlour, which offers a few child-friendly ways to make pizza fun (and is the baby of the bigger pizza parlour section later in the book) and the Crab Ravioli in Cheese Sauce – apparently making pasta at home now is just like 'cool Play-Doh'.

2.
KIDS' CORNER

HONEY MUSTARD CHICKEN WITH SPINACH MASH

This recipe works brilliantly for kids of any age. The gorgeous honey mustard chicken served with mash tweaked with spinach will get the kids eating more greens (a bit like the rice mountain on page 56). You may want to try this dish with a little less mustard at first to gauge how much your kids like it, but with the right balance of honey it is fantastic. It's a proper, family-round-the-table sort of dish.

page 56

READY IN 40 MINUTES
SERVES 4

1 onion, peeled and thinly sliced
4 skinless chicken breasts
4 tbsp honey
2 tbsp whole grain mustard
3 plump garlic cloves, peeled and crushed
3 sprigs of tarragon
150ml double cream
salt and pepper

FOR THE MASH
700g large floury potatoes, peeled and chopped into chunks
large knob of butter
80ml milk
2 large handfuls of spinach
salt and pepper

1. Preheat the oven to 180°C/160°C fan/350°F/Gas mark 4.

2. Put the sliced onion into the bottom of an oven dish. Cut the chicken breasts lengthways into 3–4 pieces about the width of chipolata sausages. Mix together the honey, mustard and garlic in a medium bowl then add the chicken pieces and stir to coat well.

3. Put the chicken strips on top of the onions, season with salt and pepper and then pour over any remaining honey mixture. Tuck the tarragon stalks in around the chicken. Bake in the oven for 20 minutes until cooked through.

4. Meanwhile fill a saucepan with just-boiled water from the kettle. Add the potatoes and cook for 10 minutes until tender all the way through. Drain well then mash thoroughly with the butter, milk and some salt and pepper. Stir the spinach into the hot mash, let it wilt then stir again to evenly disperse.

5. Once the chicken is cooked, carefully pour the juices into a small saucepan. Add the double cream and place over a low-medium heat until steaming. Taste and adjust the seasoning and balance, adding some extra mustard if necessary. Remove from the heat.

6. Divide the mash and chicken between four plates, discarding the tarragon and onions. Pour over the creamy mustard sauce and serve.

♟ VIRGIN TIP
This works just as well with pork chops but increase the cooking time so the chops are cooked through. Be sure to serve with plenty of green veg.

PULLED PORK RAGU

I absolutely love pulled pork. I started making and serving it with a barbecue sauce (which is gorgeous by the way) but here I've done something different: pork shoulder is slow-roasted and served with a delicious, homemade flavour-packed sauce and lovely ribbon pasta. This is proper comfort food and gets the taste buds going, so it will be well worth the wait! You'll have plenty left over so be sure to freeze the leftover pork and make pulled pork sliders with it another day. (I have a great video recipe for this on myvirginkitchen.com.)

**READY IN 4½ HOURS
SERVES 4**

1 onion, peeled and roughly chopped
4 garlic cloves, peeled
4–5 sprigs of thyme
750g boneless pork shoulder
3 tbsp olive oil
400ml red wine
2 x 400g tins chopped tomatoes
zest of 1 lemon
1 tbsp balsamic vinegar
1 tbsp sugar
1 tbsp dried oregano
1 tbsp chopped basil leaves
400g long pasta (I like fresh
    pappardelle)
salt and pepper

TO SERVE

rocket leaves
olive oil, for drizzling
shaved Parmesan

♟ VIRGIN TIP
Any leftover ragu mixture makes
a lovely alternative filling for
quesadillas – it's a little different,
but worth trying.

1. Preheat the oven to 140°C/120°C fan/275°F/Gas mark 1.

2. Put the onion, garlic and thyme into the bottom of a smallish roasting tin. Sit the pork on top and rub in 1 tablespoon of the oil, season the meat well with salt and pepper and pour half the red wine into the bottom of the tin. Seal the tin tightly with foil and roast in the oven for 4 hours, checking halfway through and turning the meat over so the other side is submerged.

3. Forty-five minutes before the meat is due to come out of the oven, put the tomatoes into a large saucepan with the remaining wine, the lemon zest, vinegar, sugar, oregano and basil and season well with salt and pepper. Place over a medium heat, bring to a gentle simmer and cook for 45 minutes until well reduced.

4. Once the meat is cooked, carefully remove from the tin and transfer to a plate. Discard the thyme and skim the fat from the tin, then pour the juices, onion and garlic cloves into the pan of tomatoes. Use a hand-held blender to blitz the sauce until smooth then taste – adjust with salt, pepper, sugar or vinegar as needed. Bring back to a simmer and continue to cook for 10 minutes, or until the sauce is thick.

5. While the sauce is cooking, shred the pork with a couple of forks, discarding the skin and any fatty bits. Stir the pork into the sauce and put over a low heat to keep warm.

6. Meanwhile, cook the pasta according to the packet instructions. If the sauce is getting too thick add a little of the pasta water to loosen. Once the pasta is al dente, drain and tip into the ragu, stirring carefully but thoroughly to ensure all the pasta is coated with sauce.

7. To serve put a handful of rocket on each plate and dress with oil and salt. Top with the pasta and ragu and some shaved Parmesan.

LAMB & RED PEPPER HUMMUS WRAPS

The girls love build-your-own recipes. Here we make our own easy red pepper hummus, spread it on warmed tortillas and serve with chunks of lamb that have been marinated in yoghurt; a super delicious contrast of flavours.

READY IN 25 MINUTES, PLUS MARINATING TIME
SERVES 4

400ml natural yoghurt
zest and juice of ½ lemon
1 tbsp ground cumin
1 tbsp olive oil
handful of coriander, plus extra
   to serve
600g lamb neck fillet, cut into
   even chunks
1 red onion, peeled and thinly sliced
salt and pepper

FOR THE RED PEPPER HUMMUS

400g tin chickpeas
70g tahini
juice of ½ lemon, plus extra if needed
1 jarred roasted red pepper, drained
   (or roast in advance and remove
   the skin and seeds)
salt and pepper

TO SERVE

4 tortilla wraps
roasted red peppers, cut into strips
2 little gem lettuces, shredded

1. First make the marinade for the lamb. Put the yoghurt, lemon zest and juice, cumin, olive oil and coriander into a bowl and mix thoroughly, then season well with salt and pepper. Transfer a few tablespoons of the yoghurt mixture to a separate tub and keep in the fridge for later.

2. Put the lamb pieces into a sealable freezer bag and add the rest of the yoghurt marinade. Massage it into the lamb to ensure it is fully coated, then place in the fridge for at least 5 hours, preferably overnight.

3. To make the hummus, put all the ingredients into a blender and whizz until smooth and consistent in colour, adding a little salt and pepper to taste, plus more lemon juice if you like. Transfer to a container and store in the fridge.

4. When you are ready to cook, remove the lamb from the fridge. Place a griddle pan over a medium-high heat until hot. Add the marinated lamb pieces, shaking off any excess marinade (you don't want lots of marinade on the lamb: it has already done its job of tenderising) and cook until charred, about 10–12 minutes. Cook the red onion at the same time. Alternatively, cook the lamb under a hot grill, turning until charred.

5. To serve, warm the tortillas in a low oven (or briefly char in the hot griddle pan). Spoon on some red pepper hummus, pile up some lamb chunks and charred onion, drizzle on some of the reserved yoghurt from the fridge, add some more blistered peppers, extra chopped coriander and some chopped lettuce and fold/roll/wrap however you like. The girls absolutely devour these!

♟ VIRGIN TIP
Marinating lamb in yoghurt is great for tenderising meat. You can really drive lots of flavour into it and it works a charm for chicken too. Mix it up and experiment with your favourite flavour combos.

GREEK LAMB SLIDERS

With kids and burgers (or sliders, which are essentially smaller burgers) . . . you are already on to a winner folks. Here you can introduce your children to food with a slight Greek twist with these yummy Greek-inspired lamb sliders with oregano and lemon. The kids go bonkers for these, especially as they're allowed to build their own!

READY IN 45 MINUTES
SERVES 4

600g lamb mince
zest of 1 lemon
small bunch of fresh oregano, chopped
    (or 1 tbsp dried oregano)
4 garlic cloves, peeled and crushed
1 tbsp smoked paprika
4 spring onions, thinly sliced
200g feta, sliced
splash of oil, for frying
salt and pepper

TO SERVE
8 small buns
1 baby gem lettuce, leaves separated
3 tomatoes, sliced

1. Put the lamb mince, lemon zest, oregano, garlic, paprika and spring onions into a bowl, season with salt and pepper and use your hands to mix and meld together, until combined (take care not to over-mix).

2. Divide the mixture into 8 portions about 75g each (this will give you 2 sliders per serving) and shape each into a burger, compacting together as you go so they don't fall apart when you cook them.

3. Heat a splash of oil in a frying pan and cook the burgers over a medium-high heat (or on a barbecue) for 2–3 minutes, then turn over and put sliced feta over the top of each burger and cook for another 2–3 minutes.

4. While the burgers are cooking, cut the buns in half and toast the cut sides. Lay a leaf of lettuce and a slice of tomato on the bottom, top with the burger and serve immediately.

🎩 VIRGIN TIP
If you're cooking on a barbecue, oil the bars slightly so the burgers don't stick. When you're shaping the burgers, make them slightly larger and thinner than you think you need them; they are likely to shrink during cooking.

BOLOGNESE STUFFED BAKED TOMATOES

Kids love their food presented in edible 'containers' so one way to make Bolognese a bit more exciting is to serve it inside tomatoes! This Bolognese is lovely and rich on its own, but baking it in a tomato with a cheesy lid makes it that bit more fun – give it a go! This recipe makes eight stuffed tomatoes; I usually allow one tomato per child and two each for adults, so this will feed a family of four easily, depending how hungry you are.

READY IN 15 MINUTES
SERVES 4-6

8 beefsteak tomatoes
splash of olive oil
400g beef mince
2 garlic cloves, peeled and crushed
1 onion, peeled and sliced
1 yellow pepper, deseeded and
    cut into squares
300g passata
125ml red wine
80g sundried tomatoes, sliced
1 tsp dried oregano, plus extra to serve
1 tsp dried thyme
2 tbsp grated Parmesan
handful of grated Cheddar cheese
salt and pepper

TO SERVE
green salad and garlic bread

♟ VIRGIN TIP
If the filling starts to colour too fast during baking, stick some foil on top of the tomatoes to protect them. Let them cool slightly before serving to kids.

1. Take each tomato, carefully slice off the 'lid' and put to one side. Use a small knife to cut a circle down around the top of each tomato and then use a teaspoon to scoop out and discard the flesh and seeds. Scrape lightly with your spoon around the inside to create a small tomato bowl.

2. Heat a splash of olive oil in a large frying pan and cook the mince over a medium-high heat for 8–10 minutes. Once browned all over add the garlic, onion and pepper and continue to cook for a further 5 minutes, stirring from time to time, until softened. Follow with the passata, wine, sundried tomatoes, oregano and thyme. Bring this to a simmer, season with salt and pepper and let it bubble for 10 minutes, or until the mixture thickens (you don't want it too sloppy in the tomatoes).

3. Meanwhile, preheat the oven to 190°C/170°C fan/375°F/Gas mark 5 and line a baking tray with baking parchment.

4. Remove the beef mixture from the heat and stir in the Parmesan. Fill each tomato to the top with the mixture and put on the lined baking tray, along with the tomato lids you sliced earlier. Bake for 15 minutes, by which time the tomatoes should be softened. Remove from the oven and top each tomato with some grated Cheddar cheese, a little extra oregano and some black pepper and return to the oven to melt for a few more minutes. Serve with the lids perched on top, a green salad and some garlic bread.

SIMPLE CHILLI WITH SPINACH RICE MOUNTAIN

This is a great go-to chilli recipe in my house. It's relatively mild (I'm the only one in who can do really spicy stuff), in fact it's slightly sweet from the condensed soup, but it works a charm. It's the only chilli Phoebe will eat and to make it more fun for the girls we make a rice mountain with spinach (so they get even more good stuff) and serve it with blobs of soured cream.

READY IN 40 MINUTES
SERVES 4

1 tbsp olive oil
500g beef mince
1 onion, peeled and chopped
¼ tsp ground cumin
2 tbsp mild chilli powder
1 tsp dried thyme
400g tin kidney beans, rinsed
    and drained
1 tbsp tomato purée
295g tin condensed tomato soup
300g long-grain rice
150g spinach leaves, torn roughly

TO SERVE
soured cream
grated cheese

1. Heat the olive oil in a frying pan over a medium heat and add the mince. Break it down and stir with a spatula, cooking through until it has browned. Add the onion and cook for a further 5 minutes to soften up.

2. Next add the cumin, chilli powder and thyme, stirring through to coat briefly, and then bring in the kidney beans, tomato purée and soup – pour in 200ml water at this point too. Mix until evenly combined, then cook on a low simmer for 10 minutes, stirring every so often, until the mixture has thickened considerably.

3. Meanwhile cook the rice according to the packet instructions, but adding the spinach to the rice for the last minute of cooking to wilt it. Drain thoroughly.

4. To serve this up I normally use a ramekin or measuring cup: press the warm rice into it, packing in as much as possible. Place a plate upside down on top, then flip over to reveal the mountain. Serve the chilli around the edge of the mountain with splodges of soured cream and a sprinkling of grated cheese. Delicious immediately, but any leftovers taste fantastic the next day on a jacket potato!

♟ **VIRGIN TIP**
Another quirky way to serve the chilli is in a serving glass – like you would a dessert – by stacking alternate layers of rice, chilli, cheese and soured cream. Give the kids a spoon and they'll gobble it up!

TUNA & SWEETCORN FISHCAKES WITH MINTY PEAS

The kids love making these with us; they can really get involved and have fun shaping the cakes. Smaller bite-size ones work well too. Oh and my elder daughter Phoebe normally hates peas but loves these minty peas for some reason. So, if you've got fussy eaters, give them a go!

READY IN 45 MINUTES
SERVES 4

400g mashed potato, chilled
300g tinned tuna in spring water, drained (typically 2 small tins)
2 tsp smoked paprika
3 spring onions, thinly sliced
100g tinned sweetcorn, drained
1 egg, beaten
1½ tbsp mayonnaise
100g breadcrumbs
olive oil, for frying
salt and pepper

FOR THE MINTY PEAS

200g frozen peas
knob of butter
handful of fresh mint, chopped

TO SERVE

Sweet Pepper Sauce (see page 40)
oven chips (see page 89 for my homemade chips)

1. Preheat the oven to 180°C/160°C fan/350°F/Gas mark 4 and line a baking sheet with baking parchment.

2. Find a nice big bowl and put all the fishcake ingredients, except the breadcrumbs, into it. Get your (clean) hands in there and mix until well combined, seasoning with a little salt and pepper too.

3. Tip the breadcrumbs into a shallow bowl. Shape the cakes into 8 patty shapes and then press into the breadcrumbs to coat on all sides, placing on the lined baking sheet as you go.

4. To get a lovely golden crust on your fishcakes, fry them in batches in a little olive oil until golden brown; about 2 minutes each side. Drain briefly on kitchen paper, then transfer to a baking tray and bake in the oven for 20 minutes (on the middle shelf if making chips too).

5. Meanwhile, tip the peas into a small saucepan, cover with cold water and bring to a simmer; cook for 5 minutes. Drain the peas, add the butter and mint and stir through over the heat for a few more minutes before serving.

6. Plate up the fishcakes with a good dollop of Sweet Pepper Sauce on top, the minty peas alongside and some oven chips.

♟ VIRGIN TIP
If you don't mind a softer centre, skip the baking part and just fry the fishcakes until golden brown.

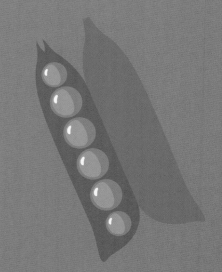

SALMON FISH FINGERS WITH PEA HUMMUS

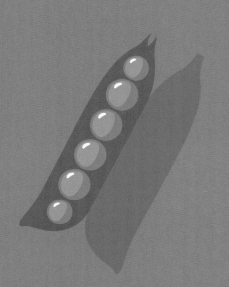

Pea hummus? I bet that's got your attention already! These Parmesan-crusted salmon fish fingers are a real winner with the kids and a nice alternative to using white fish. The pea hummus served with them is just a little tweak on a classic hummus, but it really works well. Try adding a little fresh mint – give it a go and put your own spin on it!

READY IN 25 MINUTES
SERVES 4

500g skinless salmon fillets
4 tbsp flour
2 eggs, beaten
80g breadcrumbs
20g Parmesan, grated
1 tbsp olive oil

FOR THE HUMMUS
200g frozen peas, defrosted with
    some hot water and drained
1 garlic clove, peeled and crushed
1 tbsp tahini
squeeze of lemon juice
80g tinned cannellini beans
1 tsp olive oil
salt and pepper

TO SERVE
tortilla wraps
salad leaves

1. Start with the hummus: put all the ingredients into a food processor and whizz until smooth. Taste and adjust the seasoning with salt, pepper or more lemon juice.

2. Slice the salmon fillets into fish finger-size pieces. Line everything up on your work surface: a plate with the fish pieces, a plastic food bag containing the flour, a shallow bowl of beaten egg and a plate spread with a mixture of the breadcrumbs, Parmesan and a grind of black pepper.

3. Put all the fish pieces into the bag of flour and shake so they are coated. Dip a piece of fish into the egg so it's covered, then put into the breadcrumbs, tossing until fully coated. Repeat with all the fish.

4. Heat the oil in a large frying pan and cook the fish fingers, in batches, for 2–3 minutes on each side until they are cooked through and golden. Remove from the pan and drain on kitchen paper.

5. Serve the salmon fingers and hummus in tortilla wraps with salad.

♟ VIRGIN TIP
The hummus won't be completely smooth but leave the processor running for a few minutes to get it as smooth as possible.

CRAB RAVIOLI IN CHEESE SAUCE

Making your own pasta is a doddle; it uses just two key ingredients, it tastes great AND you feel a sort of culinary satisfaction after making it. Ravioli is great fun to make with the kids too. My girls aren't keen on the idea of eating crab, but they absolutely love this dish and the cheesy sauce goes really well with it. Master the pasta and then you can put your own spin on this recipe.

FOR THE FILLING

300g tinned crabmeat, drained
150g cream cheese
1 tbsp chopped dill, plus extra to serve
zest and juice of ½ lemon
pepper

FOR THE PASTA

1 egg
pinch of salt
150g '00' flour (or plain flour)
3 tbsp chilled water

FOR THE SAUCE

2 tbsp butter
2 tbsp plain flour
250ml milk, plus extra if needed
100g Cheddar cheese, grated
30g Parmesan, grated
salt and pepper

👨‍🍳 VIRGIN TIP

As suggested in the intro, play around with different flavour combinations for fillings – veggie ones such as butternut squash or a good bolognese filling. Don't forget to let me know how you get on and send me pictures of your dishes; it's all about experimentation.

1. First make the filling. Combine all the ingredients in a bowl and stir together well. Season with some pepper, taste and add a little extra squeeze of lemon if you wish. Leave to one side for the moment.

2. For the pasta beat the egg in a large bowl, add a pinch of salt, then tip in the flour. Start mixing with a wooden spoon; it will be quite dry at first, so gradually add the water until it comes together as a dough, adding a little more water if needed. Put on to a floured surface and knead for a good 10 minutes until smooth. It may not look like much right now but this will make a fair amount of ravioli once rolled out!

3. Use a pasta machine to roll the pasta into thin sheets, starting on the thickest setting and working your way down to the thinnest setting. If you don't have a pasta machine just roll the dough out with a rolling pin on a floured surface as thinly as you can. Cut circles about 5cm in diameter from the dough, using a cookie cutter or the top of a drinking glass. Gather up the offcuts and re-roll to cut more circles. Any excess can be gathered up and rolled out again to make more circle shapes.

4. Place a small spoonful of the filling on one circle of pasta. Use a pastry brush to dampen the edges with a little water and place another circle on top to cover the filling. Crimp the edges with a fork to seal the ravioli. Repeat with the remaining circles and filling and put to one side while you bring a large saucepan of water to the boil.

5. To make the cheese sauce, melt the butter in a saucepan over a low heat, add the flour and cook, stirring, until it is combined and bubbling. Remove from the heat and gradually add the milk, stirring until combined. Return to the heat, add both cheeses and season with salt and pepper. Mix until the cheese melts; you can now tweak the sauce by adding a little more milk for a thinner sauce or continue to heat to thicken it up.

6. Cook the ravioli in the simmering water for 3–4 minutes until cooked through. Remove from the pan with a slotted spoon and serve with the cheese sauce drizzled on top, some extra dill sprinkled over and a little squeeze of lemon.

KIDS' PIZZA PARLOUR

It's only fair that the kids get their own pizza section (see pages 104–7 for the grown-up ones). I've always loved pizza (although sometimes a simple cheese toastie on a Sunday night hits the spot just as well) but the kids absolutely love them. Here are a couple of ways to serve pizzas to children to keep them fun and creative. Let them build them too, by setting up pizza stations with all the prepared toppings to hand. A pizza party can be a real rainy afternoon cure!

HAM & SWEETCORN CRUMPET PIZZAS

Serving pizzas on crumpets is so good – the holes in the crumpet soak up some of the topping – delicious!

READY IN 15 MINUTES
SERVES 4

8 crumpets
4 tbsp tomato pasta or pizza sauce
4 slices of ham, torn into pieces
4 tbsp sweetcorn, defrosted if frozen
8 slices of mild Cheddar cheese

1. Preheat the grill to high. Toast the crumpets on both sides so they are warm through to the centre.

2. Spread the sauce over the crumpets and top with pieces of ham and the sweetcorn. Top each with a slice of Cheddar and return to the grill until melted and bubbling. Allow to cool for a few minutes before tucking in.

PESTO, TOMATO & CHEESE PITTA PIZZAS

Toasted pitta bread can add a really nice crunch to this spin on pizza with simple ingredients. My girls like to make funny faces with these using courgette slices for eyes, olives for a nose and red peppers for a mouth!

READY IN 15 MINUTES
SERVES 4

4 pitta breads
4 tsp pesto (any variety)
6 cherry tomatoes, halved
40g mozzarella (or mild Cheddar cheese, if preferred), sliced

1. Preheat the grill to high. Toast the pitta bread on one side then slather the other side with pesto.

2. Scatter over the tomatoes and dot with mozzarella. Return to the grill and cook until the cheese has melted and the tomatoes have softened. Allow to cool for a few minutes before tucking in.

TENDERSTEM BROCCOLI & CHEESE FLATBREAD PIZZAS

We're taking pizzas up a notch here with some slightly more creative toppings.
The base of a simple flatbread works perfectly.

READY IN 17 MINUTES
SERVES 4

4 tbsp crème fraîche
20g Parmesan, grated
4 flatbreads
few flaked almonds (optional)
12 stems of tenderstem broccoli,
    stalks trimmed
4 tbsp peas, defrosted if frozen
black pepper

1. Preheat the oven to 180°C/160°C fan/350°F/Gas mark 4.

2. Combine the crème fraîche, Parmesan and a good grind of black pepper in a bowl. Spread over the flatbreads and sprinkle with the almonds (if using). Put on a baking tray and bake in the oven for 8 minutes.

3. Meanwhile blanch the broccoli in boiling water for 3 minutes, drain, then add to the top of the pizza along with the peas. Cook for 3–4 minutes until the cheese topping is golden at the edges and the broccoli is tender. Allow to cool for a few minutes before tucking in.

PASTA SAUCE & SAUSAGE PIZZAS

I do love alternative pizza bases, but for a really hassle-free option you can get some ready-made pizza bases and make this sausage and mushroom number. Scale it up for adults with a barbecue sauce base too.

READY IN 25 MINUTES
SERVES 4

olive oil, for frying
4 chipolata sausages
6 mushrooms, sliced
4 small ready-made pizza bases
2 tbsp ready-made pasta sauce (or use the
    Hidden Veg Pasta sauce on page 66)
100g mild Cheddar cheese, grated

1. Preheat the oven to 180°C/160°C fan/350°F/Gas mark 4.

2. Add a drop of olive oil to a frying pan and then fry the sausages over a medium heat until browned and cooked through. Throw in the mushroom slices and cook until browned. Set aside to cool and then slice the sausages into thin discs.

3. Take your pizza bases and spread with ready-made sauce. Scatter over the cheese and then add the sausage pieces and mushroom slices, dividing them evenly between the pizzas.

4. Cook in the oven for 12–15 minutes. Allow to cool for a few minutes before tucking in.

HIDDEN VEGETABLE PASTA BAKE

I've always found it a fun challenge to keep the kids guessing what they are eating. When they think that they do not like a particular ingredient, they will refuse to eat it (to be fair a lot of adults are like that too!). The girls have never really struggled with eating vegetables, but one way to load up on them is to hide them in a tomato sauce as below, it also adds considerable flavour to the dish too. You can of course make this non-vegetarian and add ingredients such as chicken, ham or prawns.

READY IN 1½ HOURS
SERVES 4

8 ripe tomatoes, halved
2 peppers (red, orange or yellow), deseeded and cut into strips
2 courgettes, sliced into rounds
1 red onion, peeled and cut into wedges
2 garlic cloves, unpeeled
2 tbsp olive oil
350ml vegetable stock
pinch of sugar
280g pasta (choose the kids' favourite shape)
50g Cheddar cheese, grated
salt and pepper

1. Preheat the oven to 200°C/180°C fan/400°F/Gas mark 6.

2. Tip all the vegetables into a very large roasting tin (use 2 trays if you don't have one big enough) and spread out evenly. Tuck the unpeeled garlic cloves in among the veg and drizzle over the olive oil. Roast for 45–60 minutes until everything is well cooked and charred at the edges.

3. Remove from the oven and squeeze the garlic cloves into the roasting tin, discarding the skins. Tip the veg and garlic into a large bowl or jug, pour in half the stock and use a hand-held blender to whizz until very smooth. Add more stock until it has the consistency of a pasta sauce. Add a pinch of sugar and season with salt and pepper.

4. You'll only need half the sauce to make the pasta bake, so set the other half aside to cool and freeze for another day.

5. Cook the pasta according to the packet instructions, drain well and return to the pan. Pour two-thirds of the retained sauce over and mix in, making sure all the pasta is well covered. Tip the pasta into a baking dish, pour the rest of the sauce over the top and scatter with cheese. Return to the oven and bake for 20 minutes until the cheese is browned and bubbling.

♙ **VIRGIN TIP**
Use the other half of the sauce for pasta, pasta bakes or as a base for soup. You can also use any veg you think you can get away with – sweet potato, squash and aubergine work well but for my kids it needs to stay tomato-coloured, otherwise they get very suspicious.

BAKED BEAN BURGERS

The kids (and us big kids) love these baked bean burgers, or 'orange burgers' as Chloe calls them. They're so simple to make using good old tinned baked beans and reserving a bit of the sauce to make a burger sauce. Make ahead and chill until you need them – although the recipe can be made from scratch in no time.

**READY IN 20 MINUTES,
PLUS CHILLING TIME
SERVES 4**

600g baked beans
2 small carrots, grated
2 large eggs, beaten
100g breadcrumbs
1 tsp smoked paprika
1 tsp dried oregano
4 slices of Cheddar cheese
olive oil, for frying
salt and pepper

FOR THE SAUCE

2 tbsp mayonnaise
2 tbsp reserved baked bean sauce
2 tsp smoked paprika
salt and pepper

TO SERVE

4 burger buns or ciabatta rolls
sliced tomatoes
shredded little gem lettuce

♟ VIRGIN TIP
Mix it up by using half baked beans, half kidney beans for a change of colour and flavour. You can also make the mixture into mini sliders or meatballs by rolling smaller.

1. Pour the baked beans into a sieve set over a bowl or jug to catch the sauce. Roughly mash the baked beans with the back of a fork in a large bowl. Add the carrot, eggs, breadcrumbs, paprika and oregano. Mix together well with a spatula until it starts to clump together slightly. Season with salt and pepper and mix through.

2. Using clean hands, take a quarter of the mixture and roll into a ball. Flatten into a patty shape, place on a baking tray lined with baking parchment, then repeat to make four burgers. Cover with another sheet of baking parchment and put in the fridge for 20 minutes to firm up.

3. Make a quick burger sauce by mixing together all the sauce ingredients and chill in the fridge.

4. When you are ready to cook the burgers, put a large dry frying pan over a medium heat and toast the burger buns with the cut side down. Remove from the heat, take out the buns and pour in a good tablespoon of olive oil. Put the burger patties into the pan and cook for roughly 8 minutes each side until golden brown in colour, adding more oil to the pan as you cook the burgers if needed. For the final minute top each patty with a slice of cheese to melt through.

5. Rest the burgers on kitchen paper then spread a little of the burger sauce on the bottom and top buns and build with the baked bean patty, lettuce and sliced tomato.

OATY BLUEBERRY & BLACKBERRY CRUMBLE

The kids absolutely love making crumbles as they can get involved at nearly every step. This recipe has a simple porridge oat topping that complements the fruit really well. Feel free to mix around the fruit in here; the girls love picking blackberries near our house so this has become a favourite.

READY IN 1 HOUR
SERVES 4

250g blueberries, washed
250g blackberries, washed
50g caster sugar, plus 1 tbsp
    for sprinkling
100g plain flour
50g porridge oats
100g butter, cut into cubes
custard or ice cream, to serve

1. Preheat the oven to 180°C/160°C fan/350°F/Gas mark 4.

2. Put the fruit into a bowl, sprinkle with a tablespoon of caster sugar and gently stir with a spatula – don't disturb the fruit too much, just make sure it is evenly coated. Tip into a baking dish.

3. Put the sugar, flour, oats and butter into a clean bowl. Use your fingers and thumbs to rub the butter into the sugar, oats and flour – this will take a couple of minutes – until the texture is fine and you can no longer feel the butter. Scatter the topping over the fruit, making sure it is fully covered.

4. Bake in the oven for 50 minutes, or until brown on top. It will be very hot when you take it out of the oven so be careful and allow it to cool for a few minutes before serving. Enjoy hot or warm with custard or ice cream.

♛ **VIRGIN TIP**
It's quite nice to add spices or other fruits to this recipe for an autumnal vibe. Adding apple slices to the fruit and cinnamon to the topping can give the dish a whole new dimension.

HOMER-STYLE
BAKED DOH!NUTS

Here's a fun way of making doughnuts in the oven without the need for a specialist pan. With a little pink icing you can recreate that classic Homer Simpson doughnut look! The kids love getting stuck in making these. Any leftover dough from the holes can be cooked as a bite-size treat!

READY IN 2½ HOURS
MAKES 15

250ml warm milk
1 tsp instant yeast
75g sugar
1 tbsp butter, melted and
    cooled slightly
1 large egg
400g self-raising flour
½ tsp salt
1 tsp vanilla extract

FOR THE ICING
150g icing sugar
pink food colouring
sprinkles

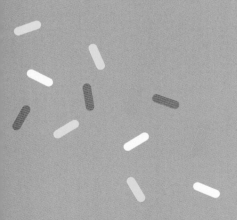

🎩 **VIRGIN TIP**
These are best eaten fresh. You could add a little flavour twist to the doughnuts by flavouring the icing with cocoa powder or different extracts such as vanilla.

1. Combine the warm milk, yeast and sugar in a large bowl. Stir until well blended and then let it sit for 15 minutes to activate the yeast. Add the butter, egg, flour, salt and vanilla and mix very well using a wooden spoon until you have a lump free dough.

2. Tip the dough out on to a well-floured surface and knead for about 3–5 minutes; it should be soft, smooth and slightly sticky. Form into a ball and put in a lightly oiled bowl, cover with cling film and leave to rise in a warm place for 1 hour, or until it has doubled in size.

3. Punch down the dough and press out on a floured surface to about 2cm thick. Do this slowly, allowing the dough a moment to spring back between stretches. Cut out circles using a 7cm round cutter. Quickly knead together the trimmings and cut more doughnuts until all the dough is used up. Transfer the cut doughnuts on to a baking sheet lined with baking parchment. Cover the tray with oiled cling film and let the doughnuts rise for a second time, for about 30 minutes. Meanwhile preheat the oven to 180°C/160°C fan/350°F/Gas mark 4.

4. To cut the holes in the centre use a 2.5cm cutter, the end of a metal piping nozzle or a bottle lid. Bake the doughnuts for 8–10 minutes until they are risen and golden and sound hollow when you tap the bottoms.

5. While the doughnuts are baking, prepare the icing in a shallow bowl. Combine the icing sugar with a tablespoon of water and a few drops of pink food colouring. Mix to a smooth paste that is evenly coloured. If you need to add a drop or two more water then do so.

6. Once the doughnuts have cooled enough to handle, dip the top half of the doughnut in the icing then put on a wire rack to drip a bit. Sprinkle with hundreds and thousands for a classic Homer Simpson look.

RHUBARB & CUSTARD CREAM DODGERS

What happens when you combine your favourite bits of your two favourite biscuits – jammy dodgers and custard creams? You get these super delicious rhubarb and custard biscuits! Ready in a flash and really fun for the kids to help make too.

READY IN 20 MINUTES, PLUS COOLING TIME
SERVES 16

110g unsalted butter, softened
60g caster sugar
1 tsp vanilla extract
110g plain flour
60g custard powder
1 tsp milk (optional)

FOR THE FILLING
75g unsalted butter, softened
150g icing sugar
1 tsp custard powder
4 tbsp rhubarb jam

♟ VIRGIN TIP
For an extra sweet layer try brushing the baked biscuits with a thin layer of rhubarb jam and baking again for a few minutes to caramelise and give sticky tops – delicious!

1. Preheat the oven to 180°C/160°C fan/350°F/Gas mark 4 and line a baking sheet with baking parchment.

2. Cream the butter and sugar together in a bowl with a wooden spoon until light and fluffy. Add the vanilla extract, then mix through the flour and custard powder. You should have quite a thick dough, so add the teaspoon of milk if you need to help it bond together.

3. Tip out on to a well-floured surface and roll out to about 5mm thick. Use a 6–7cm cookie cutter to cut the dough into circles, then gather up any excess bits and roll again to make the most of the dough. Use a smaller cookie cutter shape to take the middles out of half of the cut shapes – these will be the tops that will expose the jam later. These little offcuts can be gathered and cut or baked as mini biscuits. If you want to do some designs on the biscuits, now is the time – lightly press a fork into the cut dough edges before baking.

4. Put on the prepared baking sheet and bake for 10 minutes, or until lightly browned. Transfer to a wire rack to cool fully. Be careful not to overbake them as they will firm up as they cool.

5. Meanwhile, make the buttercream by beating together the butter, icing sugar and custard powder until you get a smooth, thick buttercream.

6. Take a biscuit bottom and spread with some of the custard buttercream. Top with a little rhubarb jam and then place a biscuit upper on top, pressing down lightly. Repeat these steps with all the baked biscuits.

RICE KRISPIE POPCORN & HONEYCOMB TREATS

I absolutely love these. Rice Krispie treats alone are a great treat to make with the kids, but adding freshly cooked popcorn to the mix with some bashed honeycomb adds a whole new dimension of texture and flavour. Give the kids a big bowl to mix this one; it can get quite messy otherwise, but hey, sometimes that's OK.

READY IN 20 MINUTES, PLUS SETTING TIME
SERVES 16

80g popcorn kernels
1 tbsp vegetable oil
100g Rice Krispies
150g honeycomb, bashed with a rolling pin (or use Crunchie bars)
100g butter
500g marshmallows

1. Line a baking tin with baking parchment (or find a deep silicone baking tray) – to make it easier to remove the mixture.

2. First make the popcorn. Put the kernels into a large saucepan with the vegetable oil. Stir with a spatula to coat them in the oil, stick a lid on top then put over a medium heat. Once the popcorn starts popping listen out for it to stop, then you'll know the popcorn is done. Remove the pan from the heat and transfer the popped kernels to a large bowl. Keep an eye out for any unpopped kernels and discard them.

3. Add the Rice Krispies and honeycomb to the bowl and mix until well combined.

4. Melt the butter in a saucepan over a low heat, then add the marshmallows. Keep stirring until the marshmallows have completely broken down and you are left with a very smooth runny white mixture, but be careful not to overheat it. Allow to cool for a minute, then carefully pour the melted mallow all over the popcorn mix in the bowl and stir together until fully coated.

5. Push the mixture into the prepared tin until compact and level. Put in the fridge for at least 40 minutes to fully firm up, then remove and slice up into 16 rectangles.

♟ VIRGIN TIP
You could shape the slightly cooled mallow popcorn mixture into ball shapes. Using wet hands, firmly press together and push in a straw or lolly stick, then coat with melted chocolate or leftover mallow mixture to hold it in place. Leave to set and hey presto, popcorn lollies!

GIANT
NUTELLA
CROISSANTS

This is one of my most requested giant foods and I've been saving it for this book – it's actually my girls' favourite breakfast treat (albeit scaled down). Making croissants can be really fun if you've got some puff pastry in your fridge, whether homemade or shop-bought. These giant Nutella croissants can be ready in a flash; perfect for sharing! You are going to share, aren't you?

READY IN 25 MINUTES
SERVES 4

2 x 320g ready-made puff pastry sheets
12 tbsp Nutella
1 egg, beaten

1. Preheat the oven to 180°C/160°C fan/350°F/Gas mark 4 and line a baking sheet with baking parchment. Remove the pastry from the fridge to bring it to room temperature.

2. Unroll the pastry on a floured surface. Ready-rolled pastry sheets are already rectangular in shape but you want the pastry a little thinner so use a floured rolling pin to roll it to a thickness of about 2mm. Take a sharp knife and cut from one corner to the diagonally opposite corner to create two large triangles. Do this with both sheets of pastry.

3. Spoon 2–3 tablespoons of Nutella on to the middle of the fatter end of one of the triangles. Now roll the pastry up starting at the fat end; roll over the Nutella and keep going until you reach the end with the pointed seam. Pull the ends in slightly towards you to make the classic curved croissant shape and press lightly to seal any gaps. Repeat with the other three triangles.

4. Put the croissants on the lined baking tray and brush well with the beaten egg. Bake in the oven for 20–25 minutes until golden brown; you don't want to burn them but you do need them to be a nice bronzed colour to make sure all the pastry is well baked. Allow to cool on the trays for 5 minutes before serving up!

🍴 **VIRGIN TIP**
You can scale down the recipe with the same sheet of puff pastry making smaller triangles to create regular size croissants, baking for slightly less time until golden brown.

SMOOTHIE FRUIT SHOTS

These are three different smoothies that we regularly mix up at home, either in standard glasses or as fun fruit shots in shot glasses. You'll notice they all use honey and yoghurt – when it comes to the yoghurt, it really helps if you get some decent quality vanilla flavour (the sort where you can see the specks of vanilla).

READY IN 5 MINUTES
EACH SMOOTHIE SERVES 4

APPLE, GRAPE & KIWI
2 kiwi fruit, peeled and white core
    removed
2 golden delicious apples, peeled,
    cored and chopped
about 20 seedless green grapes
1 banana
75ml water
180g vanilla yoghurt
1 tbsp honey

MANGO
juice of ½ orange
juice of ½ lemon
250g fresh mango chunks
180g vanilla yoghurt
1 tbsp honey

BERRY NANA
200g strawberries, hulled
juice of 1 orange
1 banana
180g vanilla yoghurt
1 tbsp honey

1. For each smoothie simply put the prepared ingredients into a high-speed blender, whizz until smooth and consistent in colour and serve.

♔ VIRGIN TIP
Including some crushed ice not only helps thick smoothies blend better, but it can also add a really nice cooling vibe on hot summer days (oh wait . . . we live in England). You have to make the most of it when the sun is out!

STRAWBERRY FLAPJACKS

This is my daughter Phoebe's recipe really – I put a Post-It note on my wall after she said, 'Remember to put my strawberry flapjacks in the book!' These classic oaty snacks have a freshly squished strawberry middle and yummy yoghurt topping. Perfect as a filler, this recipe makes a good batch of them too!

READY IN 40 MINUTES, PLUS CHILLING TIME
SERVES 18

350g unsalted butter, diced
2 tbsp golden syrup
250g demerara sugar
500g porridge oats

FOR THE FILLING
350g strawberries
zest and juice of ½ lemon
1½ tbsp sugar

FOR THE TOPPING
200g white chocolate
100ml natural yoghurt
juice of ½ lemon

♔ VIRGIN TIP
You can replace the strawberry filling with strawberry jam if fresh strawberries are not in season or if you want to save time.

1. First make the filling. Put all the filling ingredients into a saucepan and place over a low heat. Mix slowly as the strawberries break down, using a potato masher to carefully mash the strawberries into a rough, chunky texture. Remove from the heat and put to one side to cool. Once cooled, taste and tweak with a little sugar or lemon juice as you see fit.

2. Preheat the oven to 180°C/160°C fan/350°F/Gas mark 4 and line a 20cm square brownie or baking tin with baking parchment.

3. Put the butter into a saucepan over a low heat and start to melt it. When it is nearly all melted add the golden syrup and sugar and mix well. Just mix it enough so it is all combined, then remove from the heat. If your pan is big enough tip in the porridge oats and stir through; alternatively transfer the butter mixture to a large bowl and mix in the oats until fully coated.

4. Put half the oat mixture into the base of the lined tin, making sure you press it into the corners and that the surface is level. Top with the cooled jam mixture and spread out evenly. Put the other half of the oat mixture on top, again pressing into the corners and levelling off. Bake in the oven for 20–25 minutes until golden brown on top. Remove from the oven and leave to cool in the tin.

5. Meanwhile, put the white chocolate into a heatproof bowl and melt in a microwave on 30-second bursts or set over a pan of simmering water. When it has melted stir through the yoghurt and lemon juice. Pour on top of the oat mixture, spreading out to all corners. Put the flapjacks into the fridge to firm up for at least an hour before cutting up into strips. Yummy!

BABY BAKED ALASKAS

Baked Alaskas are really fun puddings, whatever the size! These baby versions are made as treats that my kids love, the charred meringue hiding their favourite ice cream on a cake base. Below are two methods: if you have a chef's blowtorch it's done in a flash, but the oven works just as well too. You can also take this up a level by colouring the meringue with food gels – mix it up!

**READY IN 15 MINUTES,
PLUS FREEZING TIME
SERVES 4**

4 brownies or pieces of sponge cake
    (ready-made or make your own)
4 small scoops of your favourite
    ice cream
3 medium egg whites
1 tsp cream of tartar
150g sugar

🎩 **VIRGIN TIP**
The trick with this recipe is patience,
especially when it comes to keeping
the ice cream cold. Prepare this in
stages and it will be a walk in the park.

1. Using a cookie cutter, cut the brownies or cake into circles and place on a small tray or chopping board. Sit a scoop of ice cream neatly on top of each one. Put in the freezer while you prepare the meringue.

2. Put the egg whites into a very clean large bowl and beat with an electric whisk until they start to create soft peaks. Tip in the cream of tartar and one-third of the sugar and whisk through until dissolved. Keep adding the sugar, a tablespoon at a time, and whisking until a glossy meringue that holds stiff peaks is formed.

3. There are two ways of charring the meringue:

Method 1: use a blowtorch
Sit the ice cream and cake bases on your serving plates and quickly coat them in the meringue, spreading it all over so it fully coats the bases with no ice cream showing. Use a wooden skewer to create spikes for a more dramatic effect. Keeping a steady distance, work your way round the meringue with a chef's blowtorch until all the meringue is toasted. Return to the freezer (if not eating immediately).

Method 2: cook in the oven
Sit the ice cream and cake bases on a baking tray lined with baking parchment. Quickly coat with the meringue as above. Return to the freezer to firm up for about 30 minutes. Meanwhile, preheat the oven to 220°C/200°C fan/425°F/Gas mark 7. Bake the alaskas straight from the freezer on the middle shelf of the oven for 3–4 minutes, or until the meringue turns golden brown (keep your eye on them). Return to the freezer (if not eating immediately).

4. Serve up on plates and wow your guests. This works exactly the same for larger size versions too: just allow an extra 3–5 minutes to brown if you're cooking the meringue in the oven.

CHOCOLATE MOUSSE
BALLOON CUPS

I'm surprised I've never done a video of this with the kids; it's part art project, part cooking. We make a gorgeously rich mousse and serve it in homemade chocolate cups shaped with the help of balloons. So much fun.

**READY IN 30 MINUTES,
PLUS CHILLING TIME
SERVES 4**

300g milk chocolate, broken
   into pieces
2 medium eggs, separated
1 tbsp caster sugar
150g double cream
grated white chocolate, to serve

You'll also need 4 small balloons

♟ **VIRGIN TIP**
You can get quite creative when
making these balloon cups: try
melting some white chocolate too.
Dunking in the white chocolate first
then the milk before resting on the
tray gives a cool finish.

1. Put half the milk chocolate into a heatproof bowl and melt, either in the microwave in 30-second bursts, or over a pan of simmering water. Transfer the chocolate to a deep bowl big enough to dunk the balloons in and put to one side for a few minutes.

2. Wash each balloon thoroughly and inflate them slightly to give a nice rounded bottom. Tie a knot in each balloon and dry it carefully. Line a small baking tray that fits in the fridge with baking parchment. One at a time dunk the balloons into the chocolate to coat about halfway up the balloon. Put on the lined tray, holding it upright for a moment so that some of the excess chocolate runs to the bottom and forms a chocolate plate for the chocolate cup to sit on. After a little while the chocolate will start to take the balloon's weight. Repeat with the remaining balloons to make four cups. Carefully transfer to the fridge to firm up.

3. Now make the mousse. Use an electric whisk to beat the egg whites until stiffened, adding the sugar and whisking for another minute until dissolved and glossy. Clean and dry the beaters of your whisk (make sure they are super clean) and whip the cream in a separate clean bowl until thickened.

4. Melt the remaining milk chocolate as before, using the same bowl used for the cups. Once melted, let it cool for a few minutes before adding to the egg yolks; stir through until combined. Gradually fold the whipped egg whites into the chocolate mixture with a spoon until combined, then fold in the cream until a rich consistent colour is achieved.

5. When the chocolate around the balloons in the fridge has set, carefully pierce them with the sharp point of a knife and remove the balloons. Pour the mousse mixture into the cups and return to the fridge for at least 3 hours to set. Serve the cups with a sprinkle of grated white chocolate on top to finish.

The most fascinating thing for me about the world of food is its diversity. I have discovered just a fraction of this from making contact with people all over the world through my videos, but there is so much more out there that I want to learn. For this chapter I wanted to feature some recipe requests that have come in or are inspired by my followers from other countries, some of whom have become friends!

You'll find a gorgeous classic Greek moussaka, the slightly less well known (unless you are Danish) Burning Love, the delicious Vietnam-inspired Banh Mi sandwich as well as a giant lamington (for sharing of course!) for the Australian in you. Each of these recipes will hopefully get you thinking about food from a different culture in a new way, and encourage you to try a new technique or two. Of course, what I really want you to do is experiment, tweak and make each of these recipes your own. The recipes are your guide, so eat the world the way you want and let me know how you get on!

3.
TASTE OF THE WORLD

GRILLED JERK CHICKEN

A Jamaican-inspired jerk chicken recipe using my own simple jerk seasoning to marinate chicken breasts, which are grilled and served with rice and 'peas' (black-eyed beans). I really love the mingling of flavours that come together in this dish; try it with skinless chicken thighs too.

**READY IN 35 MINUTES,
PLUS MARINATING TIME
SERVES 4**

1 tbsp oil
1 lime
4 skinless chicken breasts
200g long-grain rice
400g tin coconut milk
1 tsp ground allspice
1 tsp dried thyme
400g tin black-eyed beans, rinsed
    and drained
salt
chopped coriander, to serve

FOR THE JERK SEASONING
2 tbsp ground cinnamon
2 tbsp ground black pepper
2 tsp ground allspice
1 tbsp dried thyme
1 tsp chilli powder
½ tsp cayenne pepper
1 tsp ground nutmeg

1. Combine all the jerk seasoning ingredients together in a jar or Tupperware box with a tight-fitting lid and shake well to combine.

2. Mix 2 tablespoons of the jerk seasoning with ½ teaspoon of salt, the oil and the zest and juice of half the lime to make a paste. Slash the chicken breasts a few times with a sharp knife and rub the jerk paste all over. Leave to marinate, ideally for 3–4 hours but at least 30 minutes.

3. Preheat the grill to high. Cook the chicken breasts for 15–20 minutes, depending on their thickness, turning regularly. Make sure the chicken is cooked through.

4. Meanwhile put the rice, coconut milk, allspice and thyme in a saucepan with 300ml water and season well with salt. Bring to the boil and simmer for 10 minutes. Add the drained beans and return to the heat for 5 minutes until the rice is cooked and the liquid is absorbed.

5. Squeeze over the remaining lime half and stir well. Serve the rice and peas with the chicken and finish with an extra squeeze of lime and some chopped coriander.

♟ VIRGIN TIP
Keep the leftover jerk seasoning in a dark cupboard; use it for prawns or belly pork or add to a burger mix to spice up your next barbecue.

BANH MI CHICKEN SANDWICH

This is a recipe based on something I ate on a trip to Los Angeles. I was walking in the Santa Monica area and there were lots of places serving these Vietnamese-inspired sandwiches. I bought one from a street vendor with a cart and it blew my taste buds away. It's essentially a chicken sandwich with a little heat, strips of vegetables and fresh coriander. This is the closest I have come to creating the same taste.

READY IN 5 MINUTES
SERVES 4

1 baguette, cut into 4 equal pieces
8 tbsp mayonnaise
few dashes of your favourite hot sauce,
    such as sriracha
2 cooked chicken breasts, torn into
    pieces
½ cucumber, cut into batons
10 radishes, sliced
2 tsp soy sauce
small bunch of coriander leaves

1. Slice the baguette open horizontally. Spread each piece with mayonnaise and a good few dashes of hot sauce.

2. Lay the chicken on top, then layer with the cucumber and radish slices.

3. Drizzle with soy sauce then scatter with coriander leaves. Enjoy!

👨‍🍳 **VIRGIN TIP**
I'm not a huge fan of pickled vegetables, but soaking the veg in a little rice vinegar before adding to the sandwich would add a more traditional vibe. The chap I went to just sliced it fresh and I loved it. Up to you.

STICKY BBQ RIBS WITH FRESH RADISH SALAD

One of my favourite American-inspired treats – the last time I made these I remember not only how good they tasted, but how we couldn't stop laughing as the girls seemed to have as much sauce on their faces as in their tummies! Whether cooked on the barbecue or in the oven, these are absolutely delicious. The radish salad is a refreshing accompaniment. Enjoy!

READY IN 40 MINUTES
SERVES 4

120ml runny honey
2 tsp ground allspice
2 tsp smoked chipotle chilli paste
2 garlic cloves, peeled and crushed
2 tbsp dark soy sauce
1.2kg pork spare ribs

FOR THE SALAD
12 radishes
2 oranges
1 tbsp olive oil
1 tbsp white wine vinegar
2 tsp Dijon mustard
1 bag of washed watercress
salt and pepper

1. Preheat the oven to 240°C/220°C fan/475°F/Gas mark 9 or light the barbecue.

2. Warm the honey in a small saucepan over a low heat and mix in the allspice, chilli paste, garlic and soy sauce, stirring until everything is combined. Leave to cool a little then put the ribs into a roasting dish and drizzle over the sauce. Use a pastry brush to paint the sauce all over the ribs; I find this quite therapeutic and kids can help too.

3. Once the oven is hot, or when the barbecue coals have turned from orange to grey, cook the ribs for 30 minutes, turning and basting several times until the meat is cooked and the sauce is sticky.

4. While the ribs are cooking slice the radishes then cut the skin and pith from the oranges and slice the flesh into thin discs. Whisk together the oil, vinegar and mustard and season with salt and pepper. Put all the salad ingredients in a bowl and toss in the dressing. Serve with the sticky ribs.

♔ **VIRGIN TIP**
If you're barbecuing reserve some of the sticky sauce to baste
the ribs during cooking.

PINEAPPLE-GLAZED GAMMON, EGG & CHIPS

The combo of gammon, egg and chips brings back a lot of memories for me. Here a gammon joint is coated in a pineapple glaze that doubles up as a chutney. The gammon is delicious hot or cold, especially when served with oven-baked chips, fried eggs and peas. This classic continues to be a real crowd-pleaser, and what's more, you'll have plenty of gammon left over to enjoy over the next few days.

READY IN 3½ HOURS
SERVES 4

4kg gammon joint
1 litre pineapple juice
1 celery stick
1 carrot
1 onion, peeled and studded with a few
     cloves, plus a handful of cloves for
     the gammon
3 bay leaves
4 tbsp pineapple jam
2 tbsp Dijon mustard
3 tbsp maple syrup
salt and black pepper

FOR THE CHIPS
5 Maris Piper potatoes, peeled and
     cut into chips
salt and pepper
olive oil

TO SERVE
fried eggs
boiled garden peas

🎩 **VIRGIN TIP**
You can trim the rind off the gammon
at the start, but it is so much easier
to remove after boiling; it literally just
peels off.

1. Put the gammon in a very large pan and add cold water to cover completely. Cover and bring to the boil, then remove from the heat and carefully drain off all the water. Gammon can be quite salty so this step helps to remove some of the salt.

2. Top the pan up with all the pineapple juice, adding water until the gammon is covered. Add the celery, carrot, clove-studded onion, bay leaves and a good grind of black pepper. Slowly bring to a steady simmer and cook, uncovered, for 2½ hours, skimming off the foam on the top from time to time and adding more water to ensure the gammon is covered at all times.

3. To make the glaze, mix together the pineapple jam, Dijon mustard and maple syrup in a bowl. Taste and tweak to your liking. You'll only need half to baste the gammon, so store the rest in a small jar in the fridge and use as an accompaniment.

4. When the gammon is ready carefully remove from the heat and drain away the liquid. Sit the joint on a large roasting tray and preheat the oven to 180°C/160°C fan/350°F/Gas mark 4.

5. Using a sharp knife remove the rind from the joint, leaving the white fat showing. Score criss-cross lines across the top to create squares and push a clove into each square. Using a pastry brush coat the gammon well with the glaze. Bake on the middle shelf for 50 minutes, basting it at least twice during this cooking time until golden and sticky on top. Carefully remove from the oven and allow to cool briefly before placing on a board and carving up.

6. Meanwhile, cook the chips. Pat them dry with a tea towel, scatter over a baking tray and season well with salt and pepper. Drizzle with olive oil and place on the top shelf of the oven, 10 minutes after you have started cooking the gammon. Bake for 40 minutes, turning over halfway through until golden brown.

7. Just before serving cook the peas according to the packet instructions and fry the eggs to your liking. Poached eggs also work well with the yolk running over the gammon!

8. Serve slices of the gammon with the chips, eggs, peas and some of the reserved pineapple glaze in the fridge. Store any leftover ham in the fridge for another day – you'll have some great sandwiches to boast about at work, that's for sure!

SWEDISH-STYLE MEATBALLS

A little tribute to a well-known Swedish superstore which is probably known as much for their meatballs as for the flat-packed furniture they sell! I've been asked to do a video recipe on these many times, but have saved it for this book. Give these a try; I'm sure you'll love these meatballs with an onion and dill vibe and it's easier than building a cupboard!

READY IN 40 MINUTES
SERVES 4

500g pork mince (or 50/50 pork
    and beef mince)
80g breadcrumbs
1 onion, peeled and very finely diced
small bunch of dill, chopped
1 tbsp flour
1 tbsp oil
200ml vegetable stock
150g cream cheese
1 tsp Dijon mustard
salt and pepper

1. Combine the mince, breadcrumbs, onion and three-quarters of the dill in a large bowl. Season then squidge and meld the ingredients together with your hands until well combined.

2. Divide the mince into 16 and roll into small meatballs, compressing with your hands as you roll so that they stay together when cooking. Sprinkle the flour over a plate, season with salt and pepper and then roll the meatballs in it.

3. Heat the oil in a large frying pan and cook the meatballs, gently rolling and turning them until they're brown on all sides. Carefully remove the meatballs from the pan and put to one side. Pour the stock into the pan, scrape to release the browned bits from the bottom of the pan then stir in the cream cheese and mustard. Once the sauce is smooth, stir in the reserved dill and return the meatballs to the pan.

4. Cook for a further 5–8 minutes, rolling the meatballs in the sauce every now and again. Check that the meatballs are cooked through. Taste and adjust the seasoning and add a little extra stock if the sauce gets too thick.

👨‍🍳 **VIRGIN TIP**
For a true Swedish superstore experience, serve with chips and lingonberry sauce (or redcurrant jelly). These are also great served with tagliatelle.

GIANT BURRITO

In my opinion burritos – well in fact all Mexican food – are just so gorgeously simple, customisable and delicious; I think I must have some Mexican blood in me! Let's make them even more fun by supersizing them with our very own homemade tortillas, then load up with the good stuff! This recipe makes two giant burritos, each one perfect for sharing with a friend.

READY IN 1 HOUR
SERVES 4

FOR THE TORTILLAS
500g plain flour
1 tsp baking powder
pinch of salt
2 tbsp lard, at room temperature

FOR THE FILLING
1 tbsp olive oil
300g pork mince
1 garlic clove, peeled and chopped
1 green pepper, deseeded and cut
    into chunks
1 onion, peeled and finely diced
1 tsp ground cumin
150g mild salsa
150g cooked long-grain rice
large handful of chopped coriander
1 large tomato, cut into small chunks
150g Cheddar cheese, grated

♟ VIRGIN TIP
The size of these tortillas depends on the pan size so you may have some dough left over; use this to make some more regular size tortillas. You could also make the tortilla even bigger by rolling out and cooking on a very hot baking tray in the oven, in the same way as in the pizza parlour section (see page 104).

1. To make the tortillas, sift together the flour, baking powder and salt in a large bowl, then with clean hands rub the lard into the dry mixture between your fingers and thumbs until it is all incorporated. Gradually add 175ml cold water and mix through with a knife; it will start to come together and form a dough. Tip out on to a floured surface and knead for a good 5 minutes until smooth. You may need to add a little more flour if it gets sticky.

2. Split the dough in two and roll the dough out as thinly as you can. Find the largest frying pan you have and use it as a template for your tortilla: sit it on top of the dough and gently cut around the base with a knife (keep any leftover dough to make smaller tortillas later). Place the frying pan over a medium-high heat; when the pan is hot put the tortilla into it, cook until browned on one side (it is likely to puff up a bit), then flip and repeat on the other side, taking care not to overcook it. Put to one side while you cook the other tortilla.

3. For the filling, heat the olive oil in a frying pan over a medium heat, add the pork mince and cook through until browned, 10–12 minutes. Follow up with the garlic, pepper, onion and cumin, cooking for a further 5 minutes to soften. If the pan is getting too oily drain some of the oil away. Reduce the heat, add the salsa and continue to cook for 10 minutes, bringing it to a low simmer until thickened. Remove from the heat.

4. Pile up the mixture in the middle of the tortillas along with the rice, fresh coriander, tomato chunks and grated cheese. Fold in the sides, then roll completely over to seal the giant burrito in place seam side down. You can warm through in the oven if you wish or serve immediately if you can't wait!

MOUSSAKA

Goodness gracious, I absolutely adore moussaka. There is a Greek restaurant close to our home town that first introduced me to this gorgeous dish. I am actually drooling while typing this recipe so I really hope you try this deliciously filling lamb dish. The mix of spices with the texture of the vegetables really gets my taste buds going.

READY IN 1 HOUR
SERVES 4–6

2 tsp oil
400g lean lamb mince
2 aubergines, sliced
1 onion, peeled and diced
1 carrot, peeled and diced
2 garlic cloves, peeled and finely diced
1 tbsp plain flour
1 tbsp tomato purée
400g tin chopped tomatoes
500ml beef stock
1 tsp ground cinnamon
¼ tsp allspice
1 bay leaf
2 tbsp dried oregano
1 large egg
300ml Greek yoghurt
40g Parmesan, finely grated
salt and pepper

1. Heat the oil in a large, heavy-based saucepan, add the mince, and cook over a medium heat until brown. Remove from the pan with a slotted spoon, leaving behind the lamb fat.

2. In the same pan, fry the slices of aubergine until brown on both sides. Remove from the pan, drain on kitchen paper and season with salt and pepper. Add the onion and carrot to the pan and fry gently, adding a little more oil if necessary, until softened; about 5 minutes. Add the garlic and cook for a further minute. Return the meat to the pan and stir in the flour. Cook for a minute then stir in the tomato purée, chopped tomatoes and stock. Add the cinnamon, allspice, bay leaf and oregano, season with salt and pepper and bring to a simmer. Cook gently for 30 minutes.

3. Preheat the oven to 190°C/170°C fan/375°F/Gas mark 5. Beat the egg in a bowl with the yoghurt and half of the Parmesan.

4. When the mince is ready, spoon half of it into an ovenproof dish and top with half the aubergine slices. Repeat the layers and then top with the yoghurt mixture. Sprinkle over the remaining Parmesan and bake in the oven for 30 minutes until the top has browned.

🍳 **VIRGIN TIP**
This can be extremely filling, but any leftovers will freeze well – to be enjoyed another day!

LAMB BIBIMBAP

I have had tons of requests for bibimbap: a Korean rice dish that has really grown in popularity over the years. It's truly easy on the eye too, with a feast of colours going on, which is one of things that draws you to it; don't be fooled though, this dish is rammed full of flavour. It's topped with a fried egg so savour that moment when the egg yolk bursts to coat the remaining ingredients!

READY IN 25 MINUTES
SERVES 4

400g lamb loin fillet or steak, cut into strips
2 tsp sesame oil, plus extra as required
400g steamed rice
2 pak choy, sliced
8 shiitake mushrooms, sliced
2 garlic cloves, peeled and very finely chopped
8 radishes, thinly sliced
½ cucumber, cut into matchsticks
2 carrots, peeled and grated
4 eggs

FOR THE DRESSING

2 garlic cloves, peeled and very finely chopped
3cm piece of fresh ginger, peeled and very finely chopped
4 tbsp sesame oil
2 tbsp soy sauce
2 tbsp brown rice vinegar
½ tsp Korean chilli paste
2 tsp sesame seeds
2 tsp sugar

1. To make the dressing put all the ingredients into a jar with a tight-fitting lid and shake vigorously. Put the lamb strips into a bowl and drizzle over one-third of the dressing. Toss well and put to one side.

2. Heat the sesame oil in a wok over a high heat and swirl it around the pan. Add the cooked rice – don't stir for the first couple of minutes, let it sit in the pan to crisp on one side then turn over. Transfer to four warm serving bowls.

3. Throw the lamb into the wok and stir-fry until cooked through; about 8–10 minutes. Transfer to the rice bowls and return the wok to the heat, adding a little more sesame oil if needed. Flash fry the pak choy, mushrooms and garlic for a few minutes until softened, then divide evenly between the four bowls. Top with the radish, cucumber and carrot in little piles, so you have sections of colour all the way round the outside of the bowl.

4. Finally add a little more sesame oil to the wok and fry the eggs over a high heat until crispy around the edges. Add one egg to the top of each bowl and drizzle over the remaining dressing.

🍳 **VIRGIN TIP**
You can use any leftover vegetables or meat for this dish. It's traditional to have at least five different veg for nutrition and colour.

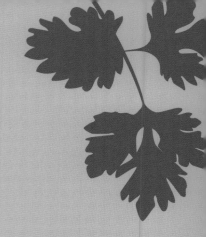

RIB-EYE STEAKS WITH CHIMICHURRI SAUCE

You get a taste of Argentina in this recipe – the classic chimichurri sauce is delicious with rib-eye steaks, making this a perfect 'date night' dinner for two – simple to create but with the flavour cranked up to eleven. The sauce goes really well with blistered peppers and onions, too as well as any barbecued meat.

**READY IN 15 MINUTES,
PLUS RESTING TIME
SERVES 2**

bunch of flat-leaf parsley
½ tsp oregano (fresh or dried)
2 garlic cloves, peeled
1 shallot, peeled and halved
½ tsp chilli flakes
2½ tbsp olive oil
juice of ½ lemon
2 tbsp white wine vinegar
1 tsp sugar
2 rib-eye steaks
salt and pepper

1. Blitz the parsley, oregano, garlic, shallot and chilli in a blender with the oil, lemon juice, vinegar, sugar and a good pinch of salt. Blend until it's finely chopped and becomes a thick sauce. Taste and adjust the seasoning and then chill in the fridge until ready to serve.

2. Take the steaks out of the fridge 1 hour before cooking so they come up to room temperature. Season both sides with salt and pepper.

3. Place a heavy-based frying pan or griddle pan over a high heat, then add the steaks. Cook to your liking: 1–2 minutes each side for rare or medium rare; 3 minutes each side for medium; 4–5 minutes each side for well done. Allow to rest on a warmed plate for 5 minutes.

4. Serve the steaks with the chimichurri sauce and some salad, a baked potato or chunky chips.

♟ VIRGIN TIP
It's really important to let the steak rest for at least 5 minutes after cooking. This will allow all the juices to settle so it won't bleed all over your plate when you cut it.

SIMPLE
COD TAGINE

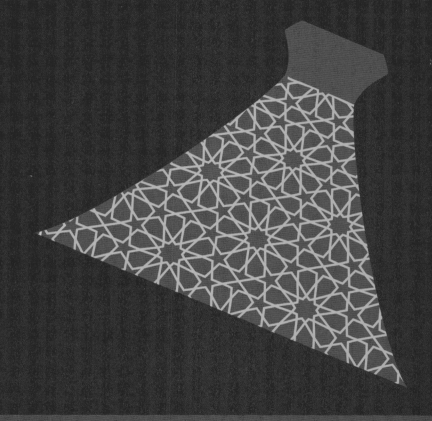

This simple, Moroccan-inspired tagine is delicious and makes a great midweek fix. Feel free to play around with the fish used in the dish here; you can also infuse the dish with other spices, such as cinnamon sticks, but the ingredients listed here tend to be ones you have at the back of the store cupboard which is why I love it so much. Ready in a flash – a gorgeous fish supper.

READY IN 25 MINUTES
SERVES 4

2 tbsp oil
3 garlic cloves, peeled and sliced
2 onions, peeled and thinly sliced
2 yellow peppers, deseeded and
    chopped
20 cherry tomatoes, halved
2 tsp ground cumin
2 tsp ground coriander
2 tsp honey
2 lemons, 1 squeezed and 1 sliced
400ml vegetable stock
2 x 400g tins chickpeas, rinsed and
    drained
500–600g skinless cod fillet (or similar
    white fish), cut into 4 equal pieces

TO SERVE
handful of chopped coriander
crusty bread

1. Heat the oil in a heavy-based saucepan with a lid and cook the garlic and onions gently for 4–5 minutes over a low-medium heat until softened. Add the peppers and tomatoes, then stir in the ground spices and honey.

2. Pour in the juice of 1 lemon, the stock and chickpeas and bring to a simmer. Lay the fish pieces in the pan and arrange the lemon slices on top of the fish. Put the lid on and cook for 10 minutes or until the fish is cooked through.

3. Scatter with coriander and serve with crusty bread.

♟ **VIRGIN TIP**
For an extra kick add some chilli flakes to the dish. If you want to try another twist on a tagine, check out the Chicken, Aubergine & Apricot Tagine in my first book *Dinner's On*.

GIANT SUSHI

If I hadn't started making recipe videos I would never have realised how much fun making sushi can be, plus it's really refreshing to eat. Here is a cool way of serving sushi in giant portions as an XL sushi roll. Serve sliced up in chunks or as the centrepiece with smaller sushi alongside!

READY IN 45 MINUTES
SERVES 4

250g sushi rice (short-grain)
2 sheets of nori (seaweed)
½ cucumber, peeled and cut into
   matchsticks
2 tbsp pickled ginger
½ red pepper, deseeded and cut into
   strips
1 avocado, peeled, stoned and cut into
   strips
200g smoked salmon, roughly chopped

TO SERVE
wasabi paste
soy sauce

1. Cook the sushi rice according to the packet instructions – this usually involves simmering with the lid on and leaving it to rest afterwards.

2. Take both nori sheets and lay them in front of you, rough side facing upwards. Use a pastry brush and a little water to dampen the end of one sheet; carefully lay and press the end of the other sheet on top. Take care and try to use as little water as possible. Put the two joined sheets to one side.

3. When the rice is fully cooled, press half of it on to the nori sheet, making sure you flatten and spread it so that it fills all the way to the ends. Use wet hands for this as the rice is sticky. Now carefully pile on the other ingredients in any order you please, spreading them out evenly. Put the remaining rice on top of these ingredients to semi-seal them in place.

4. Roll up the sheet. Use a sushi mat if you have one, but you can get by without; just keep holding it all together as you roll to firmly pack in the rice and ingredients, and keep going until you have wrapped all the way round and met the other end of the nori. Either sit the roll on the seam or cut away a little excess and use a damp finger to seal the sheet against the sushi roll body.

5. Serve the giant sushi roll cut into slices with wasabi and soy sauce to dip into.

♟ VIRGIN TIP
Play around with this concept by swapping in your favourite fillings, other meats or fish plus sesame seeds. It's sometimes nice to flavour the rice with some soy sauce or a little rice vinegar too before building; get creative folks!

MACKEREL ARANCINI

Stuffed rice balls – oh my word. This taste of the world is inspired by Italian arancini – gorgeous rolled risotto balls. Here I've given them a smoky mackerel edge that complements the other flavours fantastically to make a great canapé or starter. Once you've got the hang of making these rice balls, be creative and play around with different fillings, flavours and coatings.

**READY IN 60 MINUTES,
PLUS CHILLING TIME
SERVES 4**

1 tbsp olive oil
1 small onion, peeled and finely diced
1 garlic clove, peeled and crushed
175g risotto rice
1 large glass of white wine
750ml hot veg stock
40g Parmesan, grated
½ lemon
4 spring onions, thinly sliced
40g smoked mackerel, in small flakes
40g flour, seasoned
1 large egg, beaten
70g breadcrumbs
vegetable oil, for deep-frying
sea salt and pepper

♟ VIRGIN TIP
Rolling the risotto balls is much easier with damp hands. When your hands get too sticky, wash them and leave them damp, then continue.

1. Heat the oil in a large, wide saucepan and gently cook the onion over a low-medium heat for 5 minutes until soft but not browned. Add the garlic and cook for another 2 minutes, then add the rice and stir to coat in oil.

2. Pour in the wine and stir until absorbed. Add half of the stock and stir, then continue to stir occasionally as the stock is absorbed. Add the remaining stock a little at a time, stirring, until all the stock is absorbed and the rice is tender.

3. Stir in the Parmesan, the zest of the lemon half and a good squeeze of juice, plus the spring onions and the mackerel. Taste and adjust the seasoning. Tip the risotto on to a cold plate and put to one side to cool, then cover and chill in the fridge. Once cold shape into 12 balls about the size of golf balls.

4. Tip the flour into a shallow bowl and set it on the work surface next to a bowl of beaten egg, a plate of the breadcrumbs and a large empty plate. Roll a risotto ball in the flour then dip in the egg. Allow any excess to drip off then roll in the breadcrumbs and put on the empty plate. Repeat with the other risotto balls.

5. Preheat the oven to 140°C/120°C fan/275°F/Gas mark 1. Heat some oil in a large, deep saucepan and line an oven tray with kitchen paper. When the oil is hot (a pinch of breadcrumbs should sizzle straight away), deep-fry the risotto balls for 4–5 minutes. Cook in batches, 3 or 4 at a time then drain on the kitchen paper, sprinkle with a little sea salt and keep warm in the oven while you cook the next batch.

6. Serve with your favourite dip, such as soured cream and chive or sweet chilli sauce.

CHICKPEA CURRY

An Indian-inspired curry to please the vegans and vegetarians out there, this chickpea curry is made in a flash and is just rammed full of flavour. The chickpeas mingle with the flavours and create a gorgeously warming, yet simple dish. This will serve four as a side dish or as part of an Indian feast, so double up the quantities if you want to serve on its own as a main course.

READY IN 25 MINUTES
SERVES 4

1 tbsp oil
1 tsp black mustard seeds
1 onion, peeled and thinly sliced
2 garlic cloves, peeled and very finely
    chopped
3cm piece of fresh ginger, peeled and
    very finely chopped
1 tsp ground turmeric
1 tsp garam masala
½ tsp dried chilli flakes
400g tin chopped tomatoes
1 tsp sugar
400g tin chickpeas, rinsed and drained
2 large handfuls of spinach
salt and pepper
small bunch of coriander, to serve

1. Heat the oil in a large frying pan or wide saucepan over a medium heat. Cook the mustard seeds until they start to pop, then reduce the heat, add the onion and cook, stirring occasionally, until it is translucent and soft. Add the garlic, ginger, turmeric, garam masala and chilli flakes and stir well. Cook for 1 minute until the spicy fragrances are released.

2. Add the tomatoes and sugar to the pan, season with salt and pepper and bring to the boil. Simmer gently for 8 minutes, adding a little water if it becomes too thick.

3. Stir in the chickpeas, cook for another 2 minutes then stir in the spinach. Check and adjust the seasoning while the spinach wilts. Serve with some coriander leaves scattered over the top.

♟ VIRGIN TIP
This makes a great vegan meal for two; just serve with some flatbread to dip in.

SPANISH TORTILLA

I am a big fan of Spanish food. What I love most about this Spanish-style omelette is its simplicity. It's filling, yet light and great either hot or cold. Although there are many ways to make a Spanish tortilla, this version adds yoghurt to the beaten eggs and delicious Serrano ham. It reminds me of one the Mrs and I had on our honeymoon in Barcelona. Get creative with this and mix up the fillings – it's a keeper!

READY IN 40 MINUTES
SERVES 4

2 tsp oil
1 medium potato, peeled and cut
    into 1cm dice
1 shallot, peeled and thinly sliced
6 large eggs
3 tbsp natural yoghurt
2 slices of Serrano ham
1 tbsp pesto
salt and pepper

1. In a non-stick frying pan roughly 20cm in diameter, heat the oil over a medium heat. Add the potato and cook for 5 minutes, turning and shaking occasionally, until it starts to brown. Add the shallot and cook for a further 3–4 minutes.

2. Meanwhile beat the eggs and yoghurt together in a bowl and season with salt and pepper.

3. Reduce the heat to low and tuck the pieces of Serrano ham in around the potato. Tip the egg mixture into the frying pan, filling up all the space between the potatoes and ham, then drizzle and drip the pesto over.

4. Cook for 15 minutes until the tortilla is set on the bottom and sides. Gently loosen around the edges then hold a plate on top of the frying pan, flip the tortilla on to the plate then slide it back into the pan so the uncooked side is on the bottom. Tuck the edges in and cook for a further 5–10 minutes until it's browned on the outside and set in the centre. Serve warm or at room temperature, sliced into wedges

🍳 **VIRGIN TIP**
Great with rocket and tomato salad, it's also really nice to push the Spanish vibe even further by adding some diced chorizo – the oils released from it add a lovely smoky flavour.

BURNING LOVE

Inspired by a farmers' dish from Denmark that is well over 100 years old, this is a gorgeous filling dish of mashed potatoes with bacon and onions – perfect comfort food in winter. No one seems to be able to tell me how it got its name, which is translated from the Danish recipe name. I like it because it's about making the most of what you have. Sometimes you don't need to go flashy to make a good meal!

READY IN 25 MINUTES
SERVES 4

200g smoked bacon lardons
1 onion, peeled and thinly sliced
1kg floury potatoes, peeled and diced
50g butter
120ml single cream
½ tsp freshly grated nutmeg
small bunch of chives
small bunch of flat-leaf parsley
side salad, to serve

1. Cook the lardons in a frying pan over a medium heat until crisp. Remove from the pan with a slotted spoon and drain on kitchen paper, leaving the fat in the pan. Reduce the heat, add the onion and cook slowly in the bacon fat until meltingly tender.

2. Meanwhile fill a large pan with boiling water from a kettle. Boil the potatoes for 8–10 minutes until tender but not disintegrating into the water. Drain, return to the pan and add the butter and cream. Mash until smooth, then add the nutmeg and season with salt and pepper.

3. Divide the potato between four plates, top with the cooked onions and bacon pieces, then sprinkle over the chives and parsley. Serve with some salad on the side.

VIRGIN TIP
Add a good knob of butter to the onions as they cook if there isn't much bacon fat. Traditionally the side salad would have grated carrot so chuck some of that in if you like.

PIZZA PARLOUR

Making pizza from scratch is a real doddle, and an amazing workout! I've given you a recipe for a basic pizza dough here, as well as some advice on different ways to cook your pizza. Here's how to make five delicious homemade pizzas. Each recipe makes one large pizza to serve two people.

BASIC PIZZA DOUGH

Homemade pizza dough is something I used to avoid – it's so easy to buy ready-made pizza bases. It's fine to use these in certain scenarios, but you can really tell the difference when you make the dough from scratch, plus you can wow your guests with the stone-baked effect, which is quite easy to replicate.

500g strong white bread flour
pinch of caster sugar
2 tsp easy blend dried yeast
pinch of salt
350ml water
2 tbsp olive oil

1. Put all the dry ingredients into a large bowl and stir to combine. Add the water and oil and continue to mix well; the dough should start to come together and be a little sticky in texture.

2. Tip the dough on to a floured work surface and knead for a good 10 minutes. Give yourself a good workout, adding extra flour as needed. You can be quite rough with it. Keep going until the dough becomes smooth and elastic.

3. Put the dough into a bowl oiled with a little drop of olive oil and place a tea towel over the top. Leave to prove in a warm place for 1 hour while you prepare your toppings and preheat the oven to 240°C/220°C fan/475°F/Gas mark 9 (or the highest it will go).

4. When you are ready to use the dough, remove from the bowl and let it rest on a board for a few minutes before rolling out or shaping with your hands. You should get two large pizzas from this mix, so check out the recipe inspiration coming right up. You can also freeze any unused dough until needed.

WAYS TO COOK PIZZA DOUGH

PIZZA STONE

This is the method that gives arguably the best results. Whether you are cooking in a conventional oven or in an outdoor wood-fired pizza oven, make sure the oven is preheated as hot as it can go with the pizza stone inside. A pizza stone is basically a portable ceramic/stone cooking surface, which helps to give an authentic taste to your pizza as well as a lovely crispy base. Carefully put the prepared pizza on to your stone and cook until crisp and golden; this should take 5–8 minutes.

BAKING SHEET

Using a large, good-quality baking sheet (or a baking tray turned upside-down to create a large surface area) is a way around the pizza stone dilemma. Preheat the oven to the highest setting with the baking sheet inside so it's very hot. Once the oven has reached temperature, slide the pizza on to the hot baking sheet and cook.

🎩 VIRGIN TIP

With these first two methods, when building your pizza you can make transferring it to the stone or baking sheet easier by sprinkling a little cornmeal or semolina under your pizza dough before building.

PAN-FRIED AND GRILLED

I've done a video demonstrating this method, which has proved really popular. Get a large frying pan big enough for your pizza base nice and hot on the hob (no oil needed) and preheat the grill to high. Sit the pizza base in the pan and, as quickly as you can, build the pizza in the pan while it cooks. Cook until the pizza has puffed up and the base is lightly browned, about 3 minutes. Check the underneath by lifting it up with a spatula. Take it off the hob and place under the hot grill to finish the top, which should take a matter of minutes.

EGG, SPINACH & RICOTTA WHITE PIZZA

olive oil
2 tbsp grated Parmesan, plus extra
   to serve
4 tbsp ricotta
about 50g grated mozzarella
2 handfuls of spinach leaves, torn
3 eggs
few sprigs of rosemary, leaves stripped
ground black pepper
balsamic vinegar

1. Lightly brush the base of the pizza with olive oil and sprinkle over half the Parmesan. Place dollops of the ricotta on top and lightly spread with the back of a spoon to give an even coating, but leave a small gap around the edges for the crust. Sprinkle the remaining tablespoon of Parmesan and the mozzarella on top.

2. Scatter the spinach leaves over the base and carefully crack the eggs on to the pizza, spacing them well apart and away from the edges. Season with pepper, making sure you get some in the egg whites. Finish with a few rosemary leaves. Cook using your chosen method until golden brown and the eggs are cooked. Before serving drizzle over a little extra olive oil, balsamic vinegar and an extra sprinkle of Parmesan cheese.

DEEP-DISH HAWAIIAN

olive oil, for frying
150g mushrooms, sliced
½ x 400g tin chopped tomatoes
2 tsp dried basil
4 slices of good-quality thick ham,
   cut into small slices
200g tin pineapple slices, drained
   and chopped into small chunks
about 200g grated mozzarella
2 spring onions, thinly sliced

1. Heat a little olive oil in a saucepan and cook the mushrooms over a medium heat for 5 minutes until softened. Add the tomatoes, basil, ham and pineapple and simmer over a low heat for 25–30 minutes, stirring from time to time, until reduced and thickened. Put to one side to cool slightly.

2. Preheat the oven to 200°C/180°C fan/400°F/Gas mark 6.

3. Lightly oil a 20cm round loose-bottomed cake tin, 5cm high. Drape your rolled out pizza dough over the tin. Make sure there is enough to go up the sides and just over the top but that the dough is still thin all over. Trim away any excess dough.

4. Sprinkle the base with half of the mozzarella, spoon in the tomato mixture and spread it out evenly, then scatter over the remaining grated cheese.

5. Bake for 15–20 minutes until the crust is golden brown. Carefully remove from the tin and sprinkle over the chopped spring onion. Allow to cool for 5 minutes before cutting into wedges.

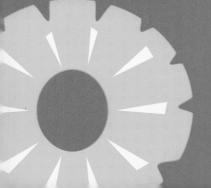

CLASSIC PEPPERONI

olive oil, for brushing
2–3 tbsp passata
12 slices of pepperoni
about 150g grated mozzarella

1. Give the pizza base a light brush with some olive oil, then add the passata, spreading out with the back of a spoon. It doesn't need to be too thick and don't spread all the way to the edges; leave a small gap all the way round for the crust.

2. Put half the pepperoni slices on top of the tomato sauce, top completely with the mozzarella, then top with the remaining pepperoni slices. Cook using your chosen method until golden brown and bubbling.

SWEET POTATO & UMAMI THIN CRUST PIZZA

1 sweet potato (about 300g), peeled and sliced into small chunks
65g good-quality rolled oats
1 medium egg
pinch of salt
pinch of garlic powder
pinch of dried oregano
2 tbsp umami paste (or tomato purée)
½ yellow pepper, deseeded and cut into thin strips
handful of tenderstem broccoli, sliced
½ small red onion, peeled and thinly sliced
60g goat's cheese

1. Preheat the oven to 200°C/180°C fan/400°F/Gas mark 6 and line a baking sheet with baking parchment.

2. Put the sweet potato, oats and egg into a food processor and whizz together until you have a smooth consistency and all the oats have been broken down. You may need to help this along by stopping the processor and scraping down the sides with a spatula. Add the salt, garlic powder and oregano, whizzing once more until well combined.

3. Spoon the mixture on to the centre of the lined baking sheet and spread out with the back of a spoon or clean hands to form a circle, being careful not to make it too thin. Bake for 30 minutes until the top forms a crust. Carefully turn the base over on to another sheet of paper so the crusted side is on the bottom. Return to the oven for a further 15 minutes.

4. Spread a thin layer of umami paste over the pizza. There is no crust here so take it right to the edge as this protects the base from burning. Add the pepper, broccoli and onion slices then crumble over the goat's cheese. Bake for another 15 minutes or until our toppings are lightly charred.

EASY ARCTIC ROLL

Ah, Arctic roll . . . a proper nostalgic taste of Britain! I never tried a homemade one as a kid; they seemed to be the buzz thing in the supermarkets and my nan would buy them frequently – essentially they are ice cream Swiss rolls. Well I've found a way to make homemade Arctic roll easy wherever you are in the world by using your favourite ice cream! The recipe below will make two rolls so you could use two different flavours of ice cream. I've given instructions for the classic Arctic roll combo of vanilla ice cream with strawberry jam.

READY IN 20 MINUTES, PLUS COOLING AND FREEZING TIME
SERVES 12

2 x 500ml cartons of good-quality vanilla ice cream
2 medium eggs
40 caster sugar, plus extra for sprinkling
1 tsp vanilla extract
40g plain flour
4 tbsp strawberry jam

1. Preheat the oven to 180°C/160°C fan/350°F/Gas mark 4 and line a 33 x 23cm Swiss roll tin with baking parchment.

2. Carefully remove the packaging from the tubs of ice cream so that you are left with two whole cylinders of ice cream. Wrap each in one layer of cling film and place in the freezer for the time being. Once wrapped in the cling film, you can shape the cylinder so it is more even, if it is wider at one end than the other.

3. Put the eggs and sugar into a bowl and beat using a hand-held electric whisk for a good 5 minutes. The mixture should go lighter in colour and double in size with bubbles appearing. Add the vanilla extract and plain flour, and fold through with a spoon until combined.

4. Pour into the prepared tin, making sure the mixture is evenly spread along the tin and is not more than 1cm thick (you may have a little mixture left over). Cut a sheet of baking parchment just larger than the sponge area and sprinkle with caster sugar, putting it to one side. Bake the mixture in the oven for 6 minutes until the sponge has risen slightly and baked through but is still pale in colour. Remove from the oven and carefully turn the sponge out on to the sugar-coated paper. Remove the tin but leave the bottom sheet of baking parchment on the sponge.

5. Roll up the sponge from one short end to the other like a carpet, with both pieces of baking parchment still in place. Leave to cool fully rolled up – this makes rolling easier later on.

6. Once fully cooled, carefully unravel the sponge and remove the paper backing. Take an ice cream cylinder out of the freezer and lay it next to one corner of the sponge; there should be room for two cylinders, so cut a line right the way down the sponge to create two long sponge strips, using the ice cream cylinder as a template. Put the cylinder back in the freezer for the time being.

7. Spread both sponge strips with a thin layer of strawberry jam. Working with one ice cream cylinder at a time, remove the cling film and sit the ice cream at one end of the sponge. Steadily roll up to cover the ice cream in the sponge; when it looks like the sponge will overlap, cut away the excess sponge (unlike a Swiss roll there is just one layer of sponge here). Wrap the whole Arctic roll in cling film before placing in the freezer until ready to serve. Repeat with the other sponge strip and cylinder of ice cream.

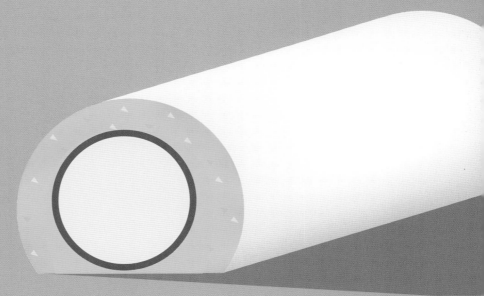

♛ VIRGIN TIP
Adding a little cocoa powder to the sponge, and then spreading it with a chocolate spread and rolling it round chocolate ice cream is a very naughty thing to try indeed – maybe you should give it a go!

GIANT LAMINGTON

Whenever I get recipe requests from Australians, a good chunk of them are for lamingtons, an extremely popular treat of small cake cubes drenched in chocolate and decorated with coconut outside. This recipe is for a giant version, to be cut up and served either in giant chunks or, staying true to its roots, in bite-size portions. Not only are these very addictive treats, they are super-simple to make.

**READY IN 50 MINUTES,
PLUS COOLING TIME
SERVES 16**

FOR THE BASE

250g butter, at room temperature
280g caster sugar
4 large eggs
250ml milk
2 tsp vanilla extract
500g plain flour
5 tsp baking powder

FOR THE ICING

140ml milk
2 tbsp butter, melted
500g icing sugar
5 tbsp cocoa powder
400g desiccated coconut

1. Preheat the oven to 180°C/160°C fan/350°F/Gas mark 4 and lightly grease a deep, 23cm square, loose-bottomed cake tin.

2. Using a hand-held electric whisk, cream together the butter and sugar in a large bowl. Add the eggs and continue whisking until combined, then tip in the milk and vanilla and whisk again – the mixture should be pretty wet. Sift in the flour and baking powder and fold through with a metal spoon. Pour the mixture into the tin and bake for 35 minutes or until it is golden brown on top and a skewer comes out clean. Leave to cool in the tin for a few minutes, then turn out on to a wire rack to cool completely.

3. While the sponge is cooling, make the icing. Put the milk and melted butter into a bowl, whisk briefly, then sift in the icing sugar and cocoa powder and whisk again until completely smooth.

4. Coat the cooled cake with the chocolate mixture; the easiest way is to put the wire rack over a tray to catch the excess chocolate dripping off. Pour generously to fully coat the top and sides.

5. Let it settle for a few moments before sprinkling coconut all over the top and sides. You may not need the whole amount; just use enough to get a nice even coat. Let the icing set with the coconut in place before serving up in massive chunks!

♦ VIRGIN TIP
You could also bake the mixture in 2 smaller tins, then sandwich together with a chocolate buttercream or jam.

GERMAN-INSPIRED SOFT PRETZELS

I remember the first time I tried supersized pretzels was at a fair, at a stall that was selling freshly made pretzels. I just could not resist them! I've gone for a classic salty edge here, but it's also popular to sweeten these with a little icing sugar – or a drizzle of chocolate is always welcome! However you make them, they are best eaten the same day, so you have a good excuse to scoff the lot!

**READY IN 1 HOUR 10 MINUTES,
PLUS PROVING TIME
SERVES 8**

500g strong white flour
7g sachet of easy blend dried yeast
25g soft dark brown sugar
1 tsp salt
50g butter, melted
3 tbsp baking powder
1 egg, beaten
1 sprig of rosemary, leaves chopped
Maldon sea salt, for sprinkling

1. Combine the flour, yeast, sugar and salt in a large bowl. Mix the melted butter with 300ml warm water and pour into the flour. Stir together to form a dough then turn out on to a floured surface and knead until the dough is smooth and soft. It will take a good 10 minutes. Form the dough into a ball, place it in an oiled bowl and cover with a piece of oiled cling film. Leave in a warm place to rise for 1 hour.

2. Line two baking sheets with oiled sheets of baking parchment.

3. Knock the dough back and divide into eight equal pieces. Roll and stretch each piece into a long sausage 2–3cm thick. To make the pretzel shapes, take one piece of dough, lay it in a U shape on the lined baking sheet, then loop each end towards the centre of the U and cross them over. Repeat with all the dough. Cover with oiled cling film and leave to rise for 20 minutes. Meanwhile, preheat the oven to 200°C/180°C fan/400°F/Gas mark 6.

4. Half-fill a large pan with water and bring to the boil. Carefully add the baking powder, taking care as it will bubble up. Lower one pretzel into the pan and cook one side for 20 seconds, then turn and cook the other side for 20 seconds. Return to the baking sheet and repeat with the other pretzels.

5. Once the pretzels have been boiled, paint them all over with the beaten egg and sprinkle with chopped rosemary and Maldon sea salt. Put the baking sheets in the oven and bake for 30 minutes.

♟ VIRGIN TIP
Check the pretzels after 25 minutes in the oven; if they have risen and the holes have closed up they may take longer to cook through. Tap the bottoms and if they sound hollow they are cooked; if they still sound dense, turn them over and cook upside down for another 5 minutes, then test again.

Food triggers strong memories. Like when you were a kid and you tried your Nan's roast potatoes and you knew that nobody else made them like she did and you can remember just what they tasted like . . . I hope you can all relate to that. So this chapter is about those dishes that make me go all misty-eyed, either because I ate them as a youngster or because they were so delicious that I have to replicate them.

There are lots of recipes to choose from, from my school dinner-inspired attempt at pineapple upside down cake (which ended in disaster on the walk home from school) to one of the first homemade dinners I tried when living out in Boston, U.S. You could even have a go at recreating my 'accidental' ultimate breakfast sandwich, which will satisfy even the strongest of breakfast cravings!

I'd love to hear any of your nostalgic food memories and, yes, I am aware that some nostalgic food is stuff that we now joke about, such as blancmange or tinned salmon pâté (needless to say that didn't make it into the book but you never know, perhaps I'll do a video on it one day for a chuckle).

4.
NOSTALGIC RECIPES

CHICKEN THIGH PARMIGIANA

I first discovered this dish when I spent some time in Boston. Back then my knowledge of food was pretty limited. I was amazed not only at how delicious this recipe was, but also how filling it was, and how quickly it was in front of me! Give this a go; it's a real crowd-pleaser.

READY IN 50 MINUTES
SERVES 4

6 tbsp plain flour, seasoned with salt and pepper
2 large eggs, beaten
100g panko breadcrumbs
500g chicken thigh fillets
vegetable oil, for frying
1 x 700g jar of good-quality passata
large handful of basil leaves, roughly torn
100g Parmesan, grated
150g mozzarella ball, cut into thin rounds
salt and pepper

TO SERVE
cooked spaghetti

1. Preheat the oven to 190°C/170°C fan/375°F/Gas mark 5.

2. Line up the seasoned flour, beaten egg and breadcrumbs in separate bowls on the work surface and have a chopping board to one side. Working with one chicken thigh fillet at a time, unroll it so it is flattened out. If any are looking too thick give them a little bash between cling film with a rolling pin so it will cook through more easily. Place the thigh in the seasoned flour, then the egg, then the panko breadcrumbs. When pressing it into the breadcrumbs give it a little push and they will grip better. Completely coat the chicken thigh all over and place on the board. Repeat until all thighs are coated.

3. Pour enough vegetable oil into a large frying pan to cover the base to about 1cm deep and place over a medium heat. Carefully cook the chicken thighs in batches for 5 minutes on each side until golden brown. Remove from the pan and drain on kitchen paper.

4. Pour half the passata into a square 14cm baking dish, then scatter over most of the basil. Scatter two-thirds of the Parmesan over this then carefully sit the browned chicken pieces in the dish. Top with the mozzarella rounds, making sure all the chicken thighs are covered.

5. Pour the remaining sauce over the chicken, season with salt and pepper, then add the remaining basil leaves and Parmesan (keep some back to serve). Bake in the oven for 30 minutes until bubbling and thickened.

6. Serve on a bed of spaghetti with some salt and pepper, the rest of the Parmesan and some torn basil. So simple, so delicious.

🏠 **VIRGIN TIP**
If you can't find thigh fillets use chicken breasts, bashed thin with a rolling pin between sheets of cling film.

FINGER LICKIN' SOUTHERN FRIED CHICKEN

Fried chicken is probably my first-choice fast food guilty pleasure. Making your own at home can be a lot of fun indeed. Working with very hot oil can be a little dangerous, but as long as you take your time and prep like you're on your own cooking show with everything laid out, this will be a breeze. The super flavour comes from my homemade spice mix, but if you have favourite spices chuck them in too! Goes brilliantly with sweetcorn, coleslaw and wedges.

READY IN 50 MINUTES
SERVES 4

120g plain flour
3 tsp soft light brown sugar
1 tsp salt
1 egg white
8 chicken pieces, thighs and drumsticks
vegetable oil for frying

FOR THE SPICE MIX

1 tbsp paprika
1 tbsp onion powder
2 tsp chilli powder
1 tsp black pepper
2 tsp garlic powder
1 tsp ground allspice
1 tsp dried oregano

1. First make the spice mix by combining all the spices in a large bowl. Add the flour, sugar and salt and mix together.

2. In a separate bowl beat the egg white with a dash of water. On your work surface lay a plate with the chicken, the egg bowl, the flour bowl and an empty plate. Having everything ready and laid out like this will work like a charm.

3. Put the oil into a deep-fat fryer and heat to 175°C/350°F. Alternatively fill a large, heavy-based saucepan two-thirds full with vegetable oil and use a kitchen thermometer. Preheat the oven to 140°C/120°C fan/275°F/Gas mark 1.

4. Dip one piece of chicken into the egg white and let any excess drip off. Roll it in the flour so it's fully coated then put it on the empty plate. Coat two more pieces of chicken.

5. When you have three pieces ready, carefully lower them, one at a time, into the hot oil (you may need to turn the temperature up slightly at this point to keep the oil at a steady 175°C/350°F). Cook for 15 minutes, turning occasionally until cooked through. Carefully remove from the oil, drain briefly on kitchen paper then transfer to the oven to keep warm while you cook the rest in the same way.

👒 VIRGIN TIP

It's important to check the chicken is cooked through. If you have a meat thermometer, it should be 73°C/165°F in the thickest part. Alternatively, slice into the chicken to make sure the meat is completely white.

ULTIMATE BREAKFAST SANDWICH

In our house breakfast with the girls tends to be cereal or porridge, but from time to time it's nice to treat yourself to a cooked breakfast. When I was growing up I would always have a bacon sandwich at the weekends as a treat before heading to tennis lessons (I have photo evidence of some truly awful shell suits!). So I've always craved bacon sandwiches, but after playing around with some leftover ingredients one morning at home I created this stonking sandwich. Sausage chunks and bacon with brown sauce and a tomato-avocado medley fused together with melted cheese on seeded bread . . . absolutely gorgeous.

READY IN 20 MINUTES
SERVES 4

olive oil, for frying
8 rashers of bacon
8 sausages, cut into chunks with
    kitchen scissors
2 ripe avocados
2 tomatoes, seeds removed and
    flesh diced
8 slices of seeded brown bread
butter for spreading
200g Cheddar cheese, grated
brown sauce
salt and pepper

🍳 VIRGIN TIP
Pressing down with the spatula will help meld the ingredients together – when you first build the sandwich it will look too high, but pressing down will compact it during cooking and then the melted cheese will hold it all together.

1. Drizzle a small quantity of olive oil into a large frying pan, add the bacon and sausages and cook together over a medium heat, stirring from time to time, until the sausages are cooked through and browned all over, 7–10 minutes. Remove from the pan and drain on kitchen paper. Drain the excess oil from the pan and when safe to do so wipe clean with some more kitchen paper.

2. Meanwhile, scoop the avocado flesh into a bowl and mash. Stir through the tomatoes and season with salt and pepper.

3. Now you are ready to assemble your first sandwich. Take one slice of bread and butter one side only. Turn it over and sprinkle the non-buttered side with grated cheese. Carefully spread some of the avocado mixture on top, place two bacon strips over that and a quarter of the cooked sausage pieces. Add a little brown sauce, then finish with another sprinkle of grated cheese. Butter one side of a second slice of bread.

4. Warm the frying pan over a low heat and lift the sandwich into the pan with the butter side facing down. Place the other slice of bread on top with the butter side facing up and press lightly with a metal spatula. Cook for 3–4 minutes until browned underneath then carefully flip over and brown the other side. Remove from the heat and repeat to make three more sandwiches. Serve with a fresh splodge of brown sauce.

LAMB SHANKS
IN GRAVY

Is there anything better than the combo of lamb and mint? They pair so well; the herby tang complementing the rich meat perfectly. Lamb shanks trigger memories of roast dinners on a Sunday – the lamb would blow me away with the textures and flavours going on. Delicious!

READY IN 2 HOURS
SERVES 4

2 tbsp vegetable oil
4 lamb shanks
1 onion, peeled and chopped
2 carrots, peeled and chopped
3 celery sticks, chopped
3 garlic cloves, peeled and crushed
2 sprigs of rosemary
1 bay leaf
2 tbsp flour
2 tbsp tomato purée
350ml red wine
1.2 litres lamb or beef stock
2 tbsp mint sauce (from a jar)
salt and pepper
mint leaves, to serve

1. Preheat the oven to 180°C/160°C fan/350°F/Gas mark 4.

2. Heat the oil in a large, lidded ovenproof casserole, add the lamb shanks and brown the meat well on all sides over a medium-high heat. Remove the shanks and put to one side, then reduce the heat to medium, add the onion, carrots and celery and cook with the lid on for 6–8 minutes until softened. Add the garlic, cook for a further minute before adding the rosemary and bay leaf and sprinkling over the flour. Cook, stirring, for a minute then stir in the tomato purée.

3. Slowly pour in the wine then the stock, stirring all the time. Add the mint sauce, return the lamb to the pan and season with salt and pepper. Bring to the boil then put the lid on tightly and transfer to the oven.

4. Cook for 2 hours until the meat is very tender. Gently lift the shanks from the sauce and leave to rest on a warm plate. Sieve the sauce into a jug, pressing the vegetables through as much as possible with the back of a spoon. Taste and add more mint sauce if you like. Serve with the sauce poured over the shanks and a few chopped mint leaves sprinkled over.

♟ **VIRGIN TIP**
If the shanks aren't completely covered by the stock when you put them in the oven turn them over halfway through the cooking time. This goes well with some mashed potato and steamed mangetout.

GOOD OLD BEEF & NOODLES

Quite simply this is here because it's a nostalgic homemade takeaway fave of mine. Beef and noodles are so simple to make at home and it probably takes as long to make as you would have to wait sitting in your local Chinese! Mix up by using lamb, prawns or chicken to keep coming back to this one.

READY IN 30 MINUTES, PLUS MARINATING TIME
SERVES 4

2 x 200g rump steaks
2 tsp sesame oil
200g tenderstem broccoli
150g green beans, trimmed and halved
600g ready-cooked or 'wok-ready' egg noodles
1 tsp sesame seeds
small bunch of coriander

FOR THE MARINADE
2 tbsp light Japanese soy sauce
2 tbsp mirin
2cm piece of fresh ginger, peeled and grated
2 garlic cloves, peeled and crushed
1 tbsp sesame oil

1. Combine all the marinade ingredients together in a bowl and whisk until combined. Add the steaks and massage in for a moment or two. Cover and refrigerate overnight, or for at least 2 hours.

2. When you are ready to cook, remove the steaks from the fridge, heat a wok with a teaspoon of sesame oil over a medium-high heat and swirl around the pan. Scrape the marinade off the steaks, reserving it for later. Add the steaks to the wok and cook for 3 minutes on each side, then transfer to a warm plate to rest.

3. Add the remaining oil to the pan and stir-fry the broccoli and beans for 3–4 minutes until they start to become tender. Add the noodles to the pan and the reserved marinade and toss well to combine and heat the noodles through. Cook for another 4 minutes.

4. Divide the noodles between four bowls. Slice the beef and put it on top of the noodles, then sprinkle over the sesame seeds and a few coriander leaves. Serve immediately.

♟ **VIRGIN TIP**
Cut any thicker stems of broccoli in half lengthways so that they cook at the same rate as the beans.

PULL-APART STEAK & CHEESE SHARER ROLLS

This recipe is super-flexible and can be tweaked in so many ways using different meats and fillings. I stumbled upon it after experimenting with leftover beef: with my love of steak and cheese subs, this tear-and-share roll recipe was born! Perfect if you want a nice filler using minimum effort and ingredients you would typically already have in the kitchen.

READY IN 35 MINUTES
SERVES 4

8 soft white bread rolls
whole grain mustard, for spreading
300g Cheddar cheese, grated
1 tbsp olive oil
1 onion, peeled and thinly sliced
5 closed cup white mushrooms, sliced
1 green pepper, deseeded and cut into
    fine strips
150g leftover roast beef or cooked deli
    beef, cut into very fine strips
black pepper
100g melted butter, plus extra for
    greasing
2 tbsp poppy seeds

♟ VIRGIN TIP
The mustard is optional – use Dijon if you like a bit more heat. When I have done this for the kids I've used ham instead of beef and mayo to replace the mustard. Play around with the concept and let me know how you get on.

1. Preheat the oven to 170°C/150°C fan/325°F/Gas mark 3 and lightly grease a 23cm springform cake tin with butter.

2. Split the bread rolls and sit all the bases snugly in the tin. (You should be able to get 8 in there but this will depend on the size of the tin; get as many in as you can.) Spread each roll base with a little whole grain mustard and put a nice pile of grated cheese on each one.

3. Heat the oil in a large frying pan over a medium heat, then tip in the onion, mushrooms and pepper. Season with black pepper and fry for a good 10 minutes, stirring frequently, until they all begin to char and caramelise in the pan. Remove from the heat (it's OK if they cool for the time being).

4. Top the cheese layer of the buns with a good heap of the cooked beef strips and follow up with spoonfuls of the charred vegetables and then more cheese on top. Place the bun lids snugly on the buns in the tin.

5. Brush the tops of the buns with melted butter and sprinkle over the poppy seeds. Cover the whole tin with foil and bake on the top shelf of the oven for 20 minutes, or until warmed through and gooey with melted cheese.

6. Remove from the oven, carefully release from the tin and pull apart the individual warmed rolls for a lovely cheesy finish!

HOMEMADE KEBABS

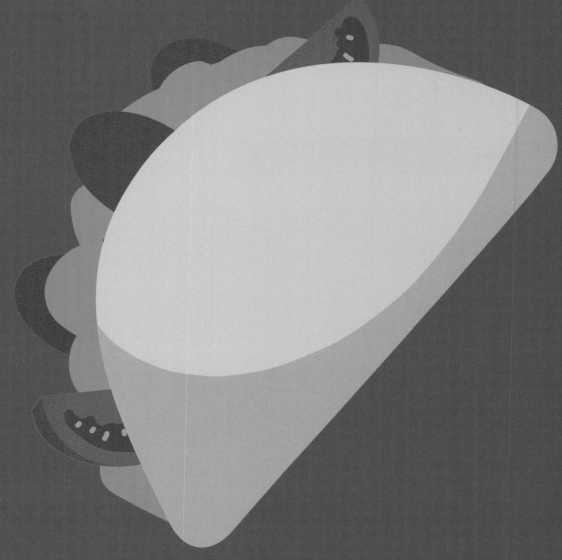

The humble kebab . . . I'm sure I'm not the only one who has fond memories of indulging in one of these after a night out – it wouldn't have been the same without one! It's so simple to make your own at home. I've opted for lamb mince here, but you could use other cuts, or even chicken or beef. Very nice indeed – even when sober.

READY IN 1 HOUR 10 MINUTES
SERVES 4

3 garlic cloves, peeled and grated
   or crushed
150ml natural yoghurt
handful of mint leaves, finely chopped
500g lamb mince
1 onion, peeled and finely chopped
2 tsp ground cumin
2 tsp ground coriander
2 tsp mixed herbs
30g breadcrumbs
1 egg
salt and pepper

TO SERVE
pitta breads
shredded white cabbage
shredded lettuce
sliced tomatoes
sliced red onion
Sweet Pepper Sauce (see Sesame
   Halloumi Bites page 40)

1. Preheat the oven to 180°C/160°C fan/350°F/Gas mark 4 and line a small, deep baking tray with baking parchment.

2. First, stir half the garlic into the yoghurt in a bowl, sprinkle in the mint and season generously with salt and pepper. Put the bowl in the fridge for the time being.

3. Put the other half of the garlic into a large bowl with all the remaining ingredients and mix to combine. Now give it a good season with some salt and pepper and mix again. If it's not completely even in colour, the best thing to do is wash your hands, roll up your sleeves and squeeze it with your hands until everything is evenly combined.

4. Press the mixture into the lined baking tray, flattening down until you have an even layer. Bake in the oven for 25 minutes. Carefully remove and drain off excess fat from the tray, then flip it over and bake for another 25 minutes. The mixture should be gently browned on both sides and, most importantly, cooked through, but to get that nice charred effect, preheat the grill to high and place the tray under the grill, then flip over and repeat on the other side. By the time the meat is done and cooked, do not be alarmed if it is about 25 per cent smaller than when you started. Slice into thin strips.

5. Serve the kebabs in warmed open pitta breads with salad, strips of lamb mince and a good dollop of mint yoghurt and sweet pepper sauce. A perfect, crunchy taste explosion – enjoy!

♟ **VIRGIN TIP**
The size of tin used to cook the lamb can affect the cooking time; for example, using a larger tin would give a very thin layer of lamb so the cooking time would be reduced significantly. If you are unsure, it's best to test a bit first to make sure no meat is pink.

EASY FISH CHOWDER

Chowder for me brings back memories of staying in New England in the U.S. and first tasting this deliciously gorgeous fish medley. This recipe is made super-easy by using fish pie mix: add extra herbs or spices such as paprika to give even more depth of flavour.

READY IN 35 MINUTES
SERVES 4

1 tbsp olive oil
1 large onion, peeled and finely chopped
100g streaky bacon, cut into small strips
3 garlic cloves, peeled and sliced
60ml dry white wine
600ml chicken stock
200g new potatoes, cut into small chunks
1 x 400g packet of fish pie mix (salmon, haddock and cod)
200g peeled prawns
300ml double cream (or use milk if you want it less rich)
2 tbsp milk
small handful of dill, finely chopped
pinch of cayenne pepper
salt and pepper
chopped flat-leaf parsley, to serve

1. Heat the oil in a large saucepan over a medium heat, then add the onion and bacon. Cook for a good 10 minutes or until the onion is soft and the bacon is cooked. Add the garlic and cook for a further 2 minutes.

2. Pour in the wine, stock and potatoes and bring to a simmer with the lid off. Once a simmer is reached, cover with the lid, then continue on a low simmer for 10 minutes to cook the potatoes.

3. Next remove the lid and add the fish pie mix, prawns, cream, milk, dill and cayenne pepper and season well with salt and pepper. Give this a good simmer for 5–7 minutes to cook the fish through.

4. Make any last minute seasoning adjustments before serving up with chopped parsley sprinkled on top. Some buttered chunks of bread with this goes down a treat.

👨‍🍳 **VIRGIN TIP**
To take things up a notch why not cut the lid off some crusty bread rolls, hollow out the middle and serve the chowder in your very own edible bread bowls – gorgeous!

TUNA NIÇOISE

Sometimes a good old salad hits the spot. I've included this in the book as I actually used to have a sort of fear of Niçoise salad – I think it was the eggs! But one day I had the chance to try it at a barbecue; I love the way the tangy dressing works with the tuna. Whip up this no-fuss classic on a hot summer day and it will be a hit.

READY IN 15 MINUTES
SERVES 4

1 large bag of mixed salad leaves
8 sunblush tomatoes, drained and
    chopped
300g new potatoes, cooked and sliced
6 spring onions, sliced
16 black olives
2 x 160g tins tuna steak in brine,
    drained and roughly broken into
    chunks
4 soft-boiled eggs (see tip below)
crusty bread, to serve

FOR THE DRESSING
small bunch of flat-leaf parsley, leaves
    picked and chopped
2 tbsp red wine vinegar
2 tsp Dijon mustard
1 garlic clove, peeled and crushed
2 tbsp capers
70ml extra-virgin olive oil
salt and pepper

1. Put the salad leaves into a large bowl and add the tomatoes and sliced potatoes. Add half the spring onions, half the olives and the tuna pieces.

2. In a separate bowl, mix together the parsley, vinegar, mustard, garlic and capers then pour in the oil while mixing. Season to taste. Drizzle the dressing over the salad and gently mix.

3. Divide the salad between four plates. Peel and halve the eggs and put two halves on each plate then sprinkle over the remaining spring onions and olives. Serve with crusty bread.

🍴 **VIRGIN TIP**
For soft-boiled eggs, bring a saucepan of water to the boil. Once bubbles are breaking on the surface, quickly but gently lower your room temperature eggs into the water. Give the eggs exactly 1 minute of simmering time, then remove the pan from the heat and cover with a lid. Give them about 7 minutes for a creamy yolk with a white that is completely set. You can play with this method and tweak to your liking as you get used to it.

Try the salad switched up with smoked mackerel; the smoky flavour can really add to the dish.

LOADED VEGGIE TACOS

The first taco I ever had was actually a vegetarian one, but I have to say I've tried a fair few since then. I get frequent requests to make veggie tacos, so here you go. I've crammed them full of delicious roasted vegetables with a little cumin and chilli kick and topped with herbs, soured cream and a dash of hot sauce – they're full of texture, flavour and freshness. I tried to make homemade carrot tortillas for this (I know, weird right?) but I just couldn't get them to work so they didn't make it into the book. Use your favourite tortilla type – wholemeal, corn, seeded, etc.

READY IN 45 MINUTES
SERVES 4

3 large ripe tomatoes, chopped into
   chunks
1 small cauliflower, cut into small
   florets
300g butternut squash, cut into bite-
   size chunks
2 courgettes, cut into bite-size chunks
2 handfuls of frozen sweetcorn
2 tbsp olive oil
1 tsp chilli powder
1 tsp ground cumin
400g tin black-eyed beans, rinsed
   and drained
juice of 1 lime
1 avocado
8 soft tortillas or taco shells
salt and pepper

TO SERVE

small bunch of coriander,
   leaves chopped
soured cream
hot sauce

1. Preheat the oven to 200°C/180°C fan/400°F/Gas mark 6.

2. Put all the chopped vegetables and sweetcorn into a large roasting tray and drizzle with the olive oil. Toss well until all the veg is coated. Sprinkle over the chilli powder and ground cumin and season well with salt and pepper. Roast for 30 minutes until everything is cooked and toasty.

3. Add the drained beans to the pan, squeeze over half the lime juice and toss. Chop the avocado into chunks and toss with the remaining lime juice.

4. Let everyone assemble their own tacos by filling the tortillas or taco shells with roast veg and topping with avocado, coriander, soured cream and hot sauce.

♟ VIRGIN TIP
Add some more chilli powder if you like it hot. Try to get a really good char/ caramelisation on the vegetables; it adds another flavour dimension. If you do fancy trying out the carrot tortilla get in touch and I'll give you some details; I'd love to see how you get on with them.

EPIC LEMON MERINGUE PIE

Is there anything better than a lemon meringue pie? I think not . . . but for this twist I wanted to indulge my mild fascination with ginger biscuits. I haven't gone too OTT with them though – a 50/50 combination of ginger biscuits and digestives. This is a real winner.

READY IN 50 MINUTES, PLUS COOLING TIME
SERVES 8

FOR THE BASE
110g melted butter
125g digestive biscuits, crushed
125g ginger biscuits, crushed

FOR THE LEMON CURD FILLING
3 tbsp cornflour
150g caster sugar
grated zest of 2 large lemons
125ml lemon juice (from 3–4 lemons)
juice of 1 small orange
85g butter, at room temperature, diced
4 large egg yolks, beaten

FOR THE MERINGUE
4 egg whites
200g caster sugar
2 tsp cornflour

🍳 **VIRGIN TIP**
If you want to pipe the meringue, fill the piping bag by standing it in a tall glass and turning back the top like a cuff. Use one hand to hold the bag under the 'cuff' while you dollop the meringue inside.

1. Preheat the oven to 170°C/150°C fan/325°F/Gas mark 3 and line the base of a 20cm springform or loose-bottomed cake tin with baking parchment.

2. To make the base mix the melted butter into the crushed biscuits and press into the base and up the sides of the tin with the back of a spoon, being sure to form a crust around the edge that will hold the filling later. Chill in the fridge while you prepare the filling.

3. Mix together the cornflour, caster sugar and lemon zest in a saucepan and slowly stir in the lemon juice. Make the orange juice up to 200ml with water and add it to the pan. Cook over a medium heat, stirring constantly, until thickened and smooth. Once the mixture starts to bubble, remove from the heat and beat in the butter until melted. Stir in the egg yolks and return to a medium heat. Keep stirring vigorously for a few minutes until the mixture thickens.

4. To make the meringue, put the egg whites in a large bowl. Whisk to soft peaks, then add half the sugar, a spoonful at a time, whisking briefly between each addition. Whisk in the cornflour, then add the rest of the sugar gradually, until smooth and thick.

5. Pour the lemon curd into the biscuit case, filling it to just below the edge of the crust. You can spoon or pipe the meringue, starting at the edges and working your way inwards. Don't leave any gaps between the base and the meringue and make sure all the lemon curd is covered, otherwise the meringue will slide off when you cut the pie.

6. Bake in the oven for 15–18 minutes until the meringue is golden and puffed up. Let the pie sit in the tin for at least 1 hour before easing out and slicing. Eat the same day – I'm sure this won't be a problem . . .

JAMMY ICED BUNS

When I was growing up I used to be fascinated with one particular bakery in my home town. Don't get me wrong – a trip to any bakery was great, but in particular I used to love what I'm going to call 'jammy iced buns' (because I can't remember their actual name). Here is my best attempt to replicate this childhood treat of freshly baked baked buns, vanilla cream and strawberries – it's pretty scrumptious!

**READY IN 2 HOURS,
INCLUDING PROVING TIME
MAKES 8**

500g strong white flour
7g easy blend dried yeast
1 tsp salt
40g unsalted butter, softened
60g caster sugar
100ml milk, warmed
2 large eggs
150ml water, at room temperature
oil, for greasing

TO FILL AND DECORATE

280ml double cream
2 tsp vanilla extract
400g icing sugar, plus extra for dusting
strawberry jam
8 sliced strawberries, plus 8 whole
    strawberries

🎩 **VIRGIN TIP**
The bakery also did a version with oranges, using marmalade and candied oranges for a topping. If you fancy giving this a go use orange juice instead of water for the icing for extra zing. For me you can't beat this strawberry version though.

1. First make the dough: put all the dough ingredients except the water into a large bowl and start to mix together. Add the water slowly and mix it as best you can with a wooden spoon, then turn it out on to a floured surface and knead for at least 10 minutes until smooth. (Or make the dough in a mixer fitted with a dough hook.) Form into a ball and put in a clean, lightly oiled bowl. Cover with a damp tea towel and leave for 1 hour to double in size. Line a couple of baking sheets with baking parchment.

2. Remove the risen dough from the bowl and cut into eight equal pieces. Roll each one into a ball, place on the lined baking trays well spread out, cover with a damp tea towel again, and return to a warm place for 40 minutes. Meanwhile, preheat the oven to 200°C/180°C fan/400°F/Gas mark 6.

3. Whip the cream using a hand-held electric whisk until thick. Fold in the vanilla extract until just combined and chill in the fridge until needed. Make a drizzleable icing by mixing the icing sugar with 3 tablespoons of water until smooth. Put to one side.

4. Bake the risen rolls for 10 minutes, or until lightly browned on top. Remove from the oven and transfer to a wire rack to cool completely.

5. Slice the rolls in half. Coat the top halves in the icing; it should be thick but runny enough to run down the sides and coat the bun. Do this on a wire rack with some baking parchment underneath and leave to firm up while you spread the bottom half of the buns with strawberry jam and top with strawberry slices. Dollop a good spoonful of the vanilla cream on top. Once the tops have set slightly, lift on to the cream and then finish with a strawberry on top! Gobsmackingly gorgeous.

PINEAPPLE UPSIDE-DOWN MUFFINS

The good old pineapple upside down cake is nostalgia food at its finest. Here I've scaled it down to gorgeous little caramelised cakes baked in muffin tins that are ready in a flash. A super-moist sponge hides that lovely cherry and pineapple layer. I once made a pineapple upside down cake at school; by the time I got home, it was an upside down upside-down cake!

READY IN 25 MINUTES
MAKES 12

2 x 400g tins sliced pineapple (you
    need 12 slices in total so you will
    have some left over)
200g soft dark brown sugar
50g melted butter
12 glacé cherries
250g caster sugar
200g unsalted butter, at room
    temperature
2 eggs
1 tsp vanilla extract
300g plain flour
3 tsp baking powder
100ml reserved juice from the
    pineapple tins

1. Preheat the oven to 190°C/170°C fan/375°F/Gas mark 5 and lightly grease the holes of a muffin tin with butter.

2. Drain the pineapple slices, reserving the juice for later. Combine the dark sugar and melted butter in a bowl and tip in the pineapple slices, carefully coating them in the mixture.

3. Put one slice of pineapple in the bottom of each muffin hole, with one of the cherries in the middle of each pineapple slice. Leave to one side.

4. Make the batter by creaming together the sugar and butter in a bowl until light and smooth. Add the eggs and vanilla extract and beat again until combined. Sift in the flour and baking powder, then pour in the reserved pineapple juice and 50ml water. Give this a good mix until the batter is completely integrated.

5. Pour the batter on top of each pineapple slice nearly all the way to the top, allowing a little room for it to rise. Bake for 13–15 minutes, or until golden brown. Check by inserting a skewer; if it comes out clean they are ready.

6. Allow to cool in the tins, then loosen the edges with a knife before serving up still slightly warm. Add a dollop of clotted cream if you are feeling extra naughty.

♣ **VIRGIN TIP**
The best way to get the muffins out of the tin in one piece is to put a wire rack upside down on top of them and flip over. Give a little tap like you would a sandcastle bucket and the muffins – complete with yummy caramelised pineapple cherry topping – should fall out.

Despite my sweet tooth, this is probably my favourite chapter in the whole book. I really enjoy taking recipes apart and adding something a little extra or unusual to them. It can sometimes raise eyebrows at first, but of course the proof is always in the eating! Quite a few of these recipes are comforting and filling, which perhaps says something about my love of substantial grub!

You'll find a really fun Mexican twist on lasagne, using strips of tortilla instead of pasta and a classic chilli filling. There's also the chorizo bolognese, which just works so well, especially those delicious smoky chorizo flavours running through it. And, of course, for those with a sweet tooth how about an absolutely incredible banana and blueberry Bakewell tart? Yep, after writing that, now I know why I love this chapter so much!

Give these a go and don't forget to let me know if you have any crazy recipe twist ideas!

5.
TWISTS
ON CLASSICS

HASSELBACK CORDON BLEU CHICKEN

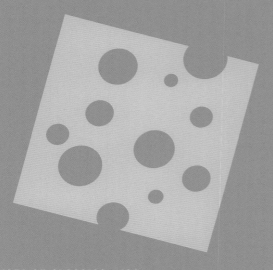

OK . . . so this recipe is just great, combining the concepts of Hasselback potatoes, chicken Kiev and chicken cordon bleu. You'll need to use quite fat chicken breasts so you can create deep pockets. The juices left in the foil after baking are great poured over the top of the chicken.

READY IN 40 MINUTES
SERVES 4

200g butter, at room temperature
1 tbsp grated garlic
30g Parmesan, grated
2 tbsp chopped flat-leaf parsley
pinch of salt
4 chicken breasts
10 slices of cooked ham, cut into
    small strips
10 slices of Swiss cheese, cut into
    small strips
pepper

TO SERVE
steamed rice and broccoli

1. Preheat the oven to 180°C/160°C fan/350°F/Gas mark 4.

2. Make the garlic butter by beating together the butter, garlic, Parmesan, parsley and salt. Keep this at room temperature for now so it's easier to work with.

3. Take each chicken breast and make several cuts along the breast, slicing almost all the way to the bottom, but leaving it still attached. Work your way along the breast to create little pocket openings. Sit all the chicken breasts on individual sheets of foil big enough to create parcels.

4. Put small amounts of the garlic butter, ham and cheese into each pocket until the chicken breasts are completely loaded. Spread a little extra garlic butter on top. Wrap the chicken loosely in the foil so it is fully sealed and make sure that the foil doesn't touch the top of the chicken.

5. Put the parcels on a baking tray and bake for 30 minutes. Leave to stand for a moment before opening up. Serve with rice and broccoli with a grinding of black pepper and some juice from the foil packets drizzled over the top.

🍳 **VIRGIN TIP**
For an added cheese boost, lay a slice of cheese on top of the cooked chicken and grill, uncovered, for a couple of minutes, or until melted and bubbling.

CURRIED CORNISH PASTIES

I absolutely love Cornish pasties. There is a bakery in my home town that makes the most wonderful pasties, which have helped inspire this twist. It's so easy to tweak the basics of a pasty – this one uses diced chicken and tikka curry flavours to create a really great-tasting pasty.

READY IN 1¼ HOURS
SERVES 8

1 tbsp oil
1 onion, peeled and finely diced
2 celery sticks, finely diced
1 carrot, peeled and finely diced
2 potatoes, peeled and cut into very small cubes
80g tikka curry paste
1 tbsp plain flour
200ml vegetable stock
2 handfuls of frozen peas, defrosted
2 cooked chicken breasts, chopped into bite-size pieces
3 x 320g packets of ready-rolled shortcrust pastry, at room temperature
1 egg, beaten

♙ VIRGIN TIP
A cereal bowl is perfect for cutting round. These pasties also freeze really well, so consider freezing them unbaked for another day. You can bake from frozen – just make sure your oven is preheated as above and allow an extra 10 minutes in the oven. You could also make mini bite-size versions of these if you like, using a glass or cookie cutter instead of a cereal bowl.

1. Preheat the oven to 220°C/200°C fan/425°F/Gas mark 7.

2. Heat the oil in a large pan and gently cook the onion, celery, carrot and potato over a low-medium heat for 10 minutes with the lid on, stirring occasionally.

3. Stir in the curry paste to coat the vegetables, then sprinkle over the flour and cook for 1 minute until everything is combined and well coated. Stir in the stock, bring to a simmer and cook for a further 10 minutes, or until the vegetables are all tender. Add the peas and season well with salt and pepper. Tip into a bowl, add the chopped chicken, stir well and put to one side to cool.

4. Unroll one packet of pastry on to a well floured surface. If necessary, roll it out a little more until it is the thickness of £1 coin. Using a bowl or plate as a guide, cut 2–3 circles about 15cm in diameter. Repeat with the other sheets of pastry then gather together the offcuts, re-roll and cut until you have eight circles.

5. Put 2 tablespoons of the filling in the centre of a pastry circle and, using a pastry brush, paint a little beaten egg around the edge of half the pastry. Fold the pastry over to make a semicircle and press the edges together. Seal by crimping with your fingers and thumb or pressing together with a fork. Repeat until all the pastry circles are filled.

6. Transfer the pasties to 2 non-stick baking sheets and carefully brush the tops with beaten egg. Bake for 25–30 minutes, or until golden brown.

TEMPURA CAJUN BACON FRITTERS – A MODERN SPAM FRITTER!

As a youngster I stumbled upon spam fritters at my local chip shop. Back in the day these thick slices of tinned spam fried in a heavy batter were very popular – they originally came about because of fish shortages during the Second World War. I've swapped the spam for some juicy bacon loin steaks in a Cajun seasoning and the heavy batter for a light and bubbly tempura!

READY IN 15 MINUTES
SERVES 4

4 bacon loin steaks
2 tbsp Cajun seasoning
olive oil, for frying
1.5 litres vegetable oil
110g plain flour, plus extra for dusting
1 tsp baking powder
pinch of salt
180ml sparkling water

1. First give the bacon steaks a dry rub with the Cajun seasoning, rubbing it into both sides. Put a frying pan over a medium heat, add a splash of olive oil and cook the bacon loins for roughly 4 minutes on each side until cooked through and browned. Remove from the pan and drain on kitchen paper.

2. Next pour the vegetable oil into a deep saucepan and heat to a steady 180°C/350°F (or to the point where a small piece of bread sizzles as soon as it hits the oil).

3. Make the batter as late as you can before dipping. Pat the bacon loins dry with kitchen paper and dust in a little flour all over. Dry loins will hold the batter better. Put the flour, baking powder and salt in a large bowl, then add the sparkling water and whisk to make the batter. Do not over whisk – just get it to a stage where it is dunkable and more or less smooth.

4. Dunk one bacon loin at a time in the batter and then put in the hot oil. Cook in the oil for 4–5 minutes, or until golden brown. Carefully lift out with a slotted spoon and drain on kitchen paper while you cook the other bacon loins.

🍳 **VIRGIN TIP**
This goes brilliantly with the minty peas on page 57 and some oven chips, not forgetting a good splodge of ketchup!

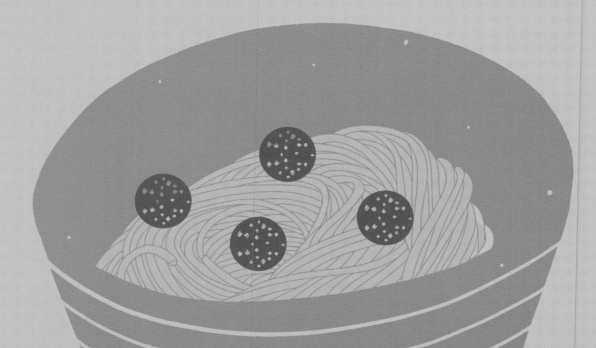

CHORIZO SPAGHETTI BOLOGNESE

Spaghetti Bolognese is a real favourite in our house. I like to make ours pretty rich in flavour anyway, but this one takes it up a notch by adding chorizo to the meat base for a smoky twist. This recipe is super-simple to chuck together – hope you enjoy it as much as we do.

READY IN 55 MINUTES
SERVES 4

1 tsp olive oil
220g chorizo, cut into small chunks
1 onion, peeled and finely chopped
2 garlic cloves, peeled and finely
   chopped
250g beef mince
220ml beef stock
160ml red wine
5 tomatoes, cut into chunks
1 tbsp tomato purée
1 tsp smoked paprika
2 bay leaves
1 tbsp caster sugar
salt and pepper

TO SERVE
400g spaghetti
grated Parmesan

1. Heat a large, deep frying pan over a medium heat and add the olive oil. First up chuck in the chorizo chunks. Stir it around the pan for a couple of minutes to start releasing the oils, then add the onion and stir through until they take on the red colour from the chorizo oil. Cook the onions for a good 5 minutes, stirring frequently, then add the garlic and cook for another minute, again stirring well.

2. Next tip in the beef mince; really break it down with your spatula into smaller chunks as you mix. Keep cooking until the mince is fully browned, then add all the remaining ingredients and season with pepper. Give it a really good stir, bring to a simmer, then reduce the heat and continue to simmer for about 45 minutes, or until the sauce has reduced down and you have a flavour-packed bolognese. Have a little taste as you go if you want to make any adjustments and remember to take out the bay leaves.

3. Meanwhile, cook the spaghetti according to the packet instructions and serve up with a fresh grating of Parmesan on top and some extra seasoning.

♟ VIRGIN TIP
This bolognese also goes brilliantly with courgetti (spiralised courgettes) instead of spaghetti – serve with a green salad for a healthy vibe.

LAMB WELLINGTON

Take beef Wellington and well, yes, as the title suggests, swap it for lamb wrapped in Parma ham – it really is stonking (sorry, I use that word a lot in my videos). Beef Wellington was always something I had a fear of making but after doing a video recipe on it, I began to experiment and this is where the lamb idea came from. Give it a go; you may find it becomes the new classic at home. You'll need to ask your butcher for this cut of meat, so think of it as a special meal for two for a special occasion.

1 cannon of lamb/loin fillet (about
    200g), cut into 2 portions
1 tbsp oil
knob of butter
4 chestnut mushrooms, finely chopped
1 tbsp Dijon mustard
4–6 slices of Parma ham
1 x 320g packet of ready-rolled puff
    pastry
1 egg, beaten
salt and pepper

TO SERVE
buttered new potatoes
green beans

♙ VIRGIN TIP
Cannon of lamb is the 'eye' piece
from a rack of loin chops – it's one of
the most tender cuts of lamb. You'll
need to order it from your butcher so
keep this dish for special occasions.

1. Season the lamb well with salt and pepper. Heat the oil in a frying pan over a high heat and sear the lamb on all sides. Set the lamb aside then reduce the heat and melt the butter in the same pan and cook the mushrooms over a medium heat for 5–6 minutes until browned. Season with salt and pepper and stir in the mustard, then continue to cook for a minute until the mixture is quite dry. Tip the mushrooms on to a cold plate and spread them out to cool.

2. Put a large piece of cling film on the work surface. Put 2 slices of Parma ham in the centre and spread over half of the mushroom mixture. Put one piece of lamb on top then use the cling film to wrap the Parma ham around the lamb. Use another piece of ham if necessary to completely encase the lamb. Roll the whole thing into a sausage shape and twist the ends so the cling film holds everything together. Put in the fridge and repeat with the other piece of lamb.

3. Unwrap the pastry and roll out further, if necessary, to the thickness of a £1 coin. Cut two rectangles slightly larger than the lamb pieces so when you put the lamb on top you will have a clear 2cm border all the way round. Cut two more pieces of pastry big enough to drape over the lamb with no gaps.

4. Unwrap the lamb portions and sit them on top of the smaller pastry pieces. Brush around the edges with the beaten egg. Lay the larger pieces of pastry over the top and bring down the sides, pressing the edges together to make a seal. Trim off any excess pastry and egg wash over the top. Carefully score lines into the top of the pastry to make diamond shapes, taking care not to cut all the way through. Chill in the fridge for 30 minutes.

5. Preheat the oven to 220°C/200°C/425°F/Gas mark 7.

6. Transfer the wellingtons to a baking sheet and cook for 15 minutes until the pastry is golden brown – this should give you lamb that is medium. Rest for 10 minutes before serving with new potatoes and steamed green beans.

PIRI PIRI SHEPHERD'S PIE

One question I'm asked all the time is: what is the difference between shepherd's pie and cottage pie? So I've ended up thinking about them quite a lot, which is where this twist has come from. I decided I wanted an alternative version of the traditional shepherd's pie. This sweet potato-topped version has gorgeous piri piri vibes running through it, which can easily be tweaked to taste as you go along. It's a real winner.

READY IN 2 HOURS
SERVES 4

2 tsp oil
400g lamb mince
1 carrot, peeled and diced
1 onion, peeled and diced
1 celery stick, diced
6 sundried tomatoes, chopped
½ tsp crushed chillies
zest of 1 lemon
2 tsp paprika
1 tsp dried basil
1 tsp dried oregano
1 tbsp tomato purée
1 tbsp plain flour
400ml tin chopped tomatoes
300ml lamb stock (or beef
    or vegetable)
1 bay leaf
2 sweet potatoes, peeled and
    thinly sliced
knob of butter
salt and pepper

1. Preheat the oven to 180°C/160°C/350°F/Gas mark 4.

2. Heat the oil in a large flameproof casserole and brown the lamb in two batches over a high heat. Once it is caramelised all over remove from the pan with a slotted spoon and put to one side. Reduce the heat to low and gently cook the carrot, onion and celery with the lid on for 8–10 minutes, stirring every now and again.

3. Once the veggies are softened add the sundried tomatoes, chillies, lemon zest, paprika, basil and oregano. Stir well and cook for a minute or two until the spices become aromatic – your kitchen should smell great. Return the lamb to the pan and stir together. Mix in the tomato purée then stir in the flour, cook for a minute and add the tomatoes and stock. Add the bay leaf, season with salt and pepper and bring to a simmer.

4. Remove from the heat and start putting the sweet potato slices over the top so that they overlap. Dot with the butter and season with salt and pepper. Bake, uncovered, for 1 hour, or until the potatoes are cooked and crisping at the edges.

👨‍🍳 VIRGIN TIP
To make this even more substantial and filling, try serving with some cornbread. You can also make individual portions by baking in smaller dishes.

MEXICAN LASAGNE

Fusing two of my favourite things – Mexican food and lasagne – was a no-brainer. It takes a little time to bring it all together, but it's worth it and the kids love it. Tweak this to your liking – it makes a medium to mild chilli but use hot chilli powder or add sliced jalapeños for extra heat!

READY IN 3 HOURS
SERVES 4

1 tbsp olive oil

400g lean beef mince

1 onion, peeled and finely chopped

1 carrot, peeled and finely chopped

3 garlic cloves, peeled and crushed

1 red pepper, deseeded and finely chopped

2 tsp chilli powder

2 tsp ground cumin

1 tsp smoked paprika

2 tsp ground coriander

2 tsp good-quality cocoa powder

2 tbsp tomato purée

2 bay leaves

400ml beef stock

400g tin chopped tomatoes

400g tin red kidney beans, rinsed and drained

300g natural yoghurt

1 egg, beaten

50g grated Parmesan, plus extra for the top

3 spring onions, thinly sliced

6 flour tortillas

salt and pepper

TO SERVE
coriander leaves
green salad

1. Heat the oil in a large saucepan over a medium heat and brown the meat. Remove with a slotted spoon and put to one side. Reduce the heat to low, add the onion and carrot, stir and put on the lid. Sweat for 10 minutes, adding water if needed to prevent it catching on the bottom. Add the garlic and cook for a minute.

2. Add the red pepper and cook for another minute. Stir in the ground spices, cocoa powder and tomato purée and throw in the bay leaves. Return the browned mince to the pan along with any juices, stir well to combine everything then add the stock and tomatoes. Season with salt and pepper and stir together. Bring back to a simmer and cook gently for 2 hours, stirring occasionally.

3. After 2 hours the chilli will be thick and rich. Add the kidney beans and heat for 10 minutes. Taste and adjust the seasoning and remove the bay leaves.

4. Meanwhile, put the yoghurt, egg, Parmesan and spring onions into a bowl, mix to combine and season with salt and pepper. Preheat the oven to 180°C/160°C fan/350°F/Gas mark 4.

5. Spoon one-third of the chilli into an oven dish. Rip the tortillas into halves or strips to fit the dish, then layer over the chilli. Spread or dollop over one-third of the yoghurt mix then repeat the layers twice more, finishing with yoghurt mix. Add an extra sprinkle of Parmesan over the top then bake for 30 minutes.

6. Use a sharp knife to cut pieces of 'lasagne' and serve with a side salad and a few coriander leaves.

♟ VIRGIN TIP
Brown the meat in a thin layer in a hot pan until caramelised on one side, then turn. Cook in two batches if necessary; overcrowding the pan prevents you getting a good colour.

VEGGIE SAUSAGE ROLLS WITH CARAMELISED ONION CHUTNEY

Sausage rolls are an all-time favourite of mine, but amazingly many of my international viewers have never heard of them. A video is coming soon! I've tweaked this picnic snack to make them veggie and coated with sesame seeds, served with caramelised onion chutney. The flavours and textures work so well together. The chutney recipe makes about three jars, but it keeps for a year and is really versatile.

READY IN 1 HOUR 10 MINUTES
MAKES 8 LARGE OR 16 SMALL

FOR THE CHUTNEY

3 tbsp olive oil
1.5kg onions, peeled and thinly sliced
280g soft dark brown sugar
200ml cider vinegar
3 garlic cloves, peeled and crushed
2 tsp whole grain mustard
½ tsp salt
¼ tsp paprika

FOR THE VEGGIE ROLLS

1 onion, peeled and quartered
3 garlic cloves, peeled
400g tin butter beans, rinsed
    and drained
400g tin cannellini beans, rinsed
    and drained
400g tin puy lentils, rinsed and drained
1 tbsp Marmite (or other yeast extract)
80g Cheddar cheese, grated
1 x 320g packet of ready-rolled
    puff pastry
1 egg, beaten
1 tbsp sesame seeds
salt and pepper

1. Start with the chutney. Gently heat the oil in a large pan and soften the onions for 10 minutes with the lid on, stirring occasionally to stop them browning. Stir in 3 tablespoons of sugar and turn up the heat to caramelise and brown the onions -- but don't let them burn. Add the remaining sugar, vinegar, garlic, mustard, salt and paprika. Simmer for 15 minutes until thickened.

2. Allow to cool before spooning into three 250ml sterilised jars. Use one jar to serve with your veggie rolls; keep the other two to mature for a couple of weeks.

3. Meanwhile, make the veggie rolls. Preheat the oven to 200°C/180°C fan/400°F/Gas mark 6. Whizz the onion and garlic in a food processor or blender until finely chopped. Add the beans, lentils and Marmite and blend again, stopping while the mixture still has texture. Add the cheese, season, scrape down the sides of the bowl and pulse to mix in the cheese.

4. Roll out the unwrapped pastry on a lightly floured work surface to make the rectangle a little wider. Cut in half and trim to make two long rectangles. Spoon the bean mix in a line about 2cm from the front of each pastry strip. Brush beaten egg along the front pastry edge, then fold the pastry over and press down on the eggy strip. Crimp the edges together with a fork. Brush the top with more egg, then sprinkle with sesame seeds. Cut each roll into four large or eight small pieces and transfer to a non-stick baking sheet. Bake for 22–25 minutes until puffed up and golden.

♟ VIRGIN TIP
Freeze any sausage rolls you don't use before baking, or make a double batch and freeze to enjoy later.

MAC 'N' CHEESE

Macaroni cheese gets a fun little upgrade in this dish with the addition of poached smoked mackerel fillets. This is a perfect tummy filler that the whole family enjoys, so mix it up and try the recipe with other types of fish such as cod.

READY IN 55 MINUTES
SERVES 6

300g macaroni
1 tbsp olive oil
1 onion, peeled and thinly sliced
1 courgette, quartered lengthways
    and then sliced
3 tbsp butter
3 tbsp plain flour
600ml milk
250g smoked mackerel fillets, flaked
350g Cheddar cheese, grated
1 egg, beaten
100g breadcrumbs
salt and pepper

1. Preheat the oven to 180°C/160°C fan/350°F/Gas mark 4.

2. Bring a large saucepan of salted water to the boil and cook the macaroni according to the packet instructions. Drain and put to one side.

3. Heat the olive oil in a frying pan over a medium heat and gently fry the onion and courgette until softened and the onions are just starting to caramelise; about 5 minutes. Leave to one side.

4. Now make the sauce. Melt the butter in a large saucepan over a low heat and whisk in the flour; keep it moving until fully combined then whisk over the heat for another minute or two. Gradually add the milk, stirring all the time, then add the flaked mackerel and onion and courgette mixture. Simmer gently for 5 minutes, stirring from time to time. Season to taste with salt and pepper.

5. Remove from the heat and add the grated cheese and macaroni, stirring through until the pasta is coated in the sauce. Finally pour in the beaten egg a little at a time. Tip the mixture into a deep baking dish and spread so it is level. Sprinkle the breadcrumbs over the top and bake for 25 minutes, or until golden brown on top. Let it cool slightly before serving.

👨‍🍳 **VIRGIN TIP**
I really like to increase the smoked element of the dish by swapping a third of the Cheddar cheese for some smoked Cheddar too. You could also add a few strips of cheese before the breadcrumb layer on top for an extra cheesy surprise!

POSH PIGS IN BLANKETS

I wanted to take one of my guilty pleasure foods at Christmas and add a little extra something. Seriously, if Christmas dinner was just a plate of pigs in blankets I wouldn't complain; but these pancetta-wrapped chipolatas with cranberry dip would probably take me into the New Year too!

READY IN 25 MINUTES
MAKES 12

12 pork chipolatas
12 slices of pancetta
1 tbsp runny honey
1 tbsp whole grain mustard

FOR THE DIP
1 x 200g jar of cranberry sauce
1 orange
¼ tsp allspice

1. Preheat the oven to 200°C/180°C fan/400°F/Gas mark 6.

2. Wrap each sausage in pancetta and put them into a non-stick baking tray, seam side down so they don't unroll when cooked. Cook in the oven for 15 minutes.

3. Meanwhile, make the dip. Put the cranberry sauce into a small saucepan with the zest of the whole orange and the juice of half. Add the allspice and stir together over a low heat. Once warm pour into a dish.

4. Mix together the honey and mustard in a small bowl. When the sausages have been in the oven for 15 minutes, brush the honey and mustard over them and return to the oven for 5 minutes. Remove from the oven and brush over any unused honey and mustard. Leave to cool for a few minutes before serving with the cranberry dip.

🎩 **VIRGIN TIP**
These make a fantastic alternative or upgrade to your Christmas dinner.
If you try them don't forget to send a picture of your attempt!

SEA BASS WITH LIME BROWNED BUTTER AND PEACH SALSA

I love experimenting with sea bass – it's such a great fish. Here I've made a flavourful butter and a lime peach salsa to accompany gorgeous sea bass fillets. The crushed potatoes really add something to the presentation. I love this dish!

READY IN 40 MINUTES
SERVES 2

350g new potatoes
40g butter
juice of ½ lime, plus extra for
    squeezing over
2 tsp oil
2 or 4 sea bass fillets (depending
    on their size), skin on
salt and pepper

FOR THE SALSA

1 ripe peach or nectarine
¼ red chilli, deseeded and finely diced
1 shallot, peeled and finely diced
zest and juice of ½ lime
½ tsp sugar
small bunch of coriander, chopped

♔ VIRGIN TIP
When cooking the fish, gently press the fillets down in the frying pan to stop them curling up.

1. First make the salsa. Remove the stone from the peach and chop the flesh into small chunks. Add to a bowl with the other salsa ingredients and toss until combined. Cover and leave to macerate in the fridge.

2. Boil a kettle of water, use it to fill a saucepan and simmer the potatoes for 15 minutes (depending on their size) until tender and cooked.

3. While the potatoes are cooking, melt the butter in a small saucepan. Once melted it will begin to foam and come up the sides of the pan and you'll start to see nutty brown spots appear; allow the butter to go golden brown to intensify the flavour then turn off the heat so it doesn't burn. Leave to cool for a few seconds then add the lime juice. Swirl the pan to mix them together, then put to one side.

4. Heat the oil in a large non-stick frying pan. Cook the sea bass, skin side down, over a medium-high heat for 4–5 minutes, until the skin is crisp and the fish is almost cooked through. Turn the fillets over for the final 30 seconds. Remove from the heat and squeeze over some lime.

5. Drain the potatoes and gently crush them with a potato masher so they are smashed rather than mashed. Give the browned butter a quick whisk and stir a couple of spoonfuls through the potatoes. Taste and season with salt and pepper.

6. Drizzle the fish with the remaining browned butter and serve with the potatoes and a couple of spoonfuls of peach salsa.

PEACH AND PEAR MELBA

I've still got a photo of a family holiday in Tenerife which shows me eating a peach melba – it was the first time I had come across this amazing combination of peaches in raspberry sauce and ice cream. For this recipe I've used pears and added a little elderflower to the poaching mix, as well as some bashed meringue for texture. Considering how impressive it looks, it's a very simple dessert to make!

READY IN 40 MINUTES
SERVES 4

250ml elderflower cordial, plus
   1½ tbsp for the sauce
5 tbsp caster sugar
2 ripe pears, washed
2 ripe peaches, washed
250g raspberries, washed
3 tbsp icing sugar

TO SERVE
vanilla ice cream
2 meringue nests, bashed
handful of chopped hazelnuts

1. Put the elderflower cordial into a large saucepan with 750ml water and the caster sugar. Place over a low heat and stir until dissolved. Add the whole pears and peaches to the pan and bring up to a steady simmer. Keep the fruit on a simmer until fully softened – this should take 25–30 minutes. You'll be able to tell when it's done as the skin will have some slight movement in it.

2. Meanwhile, put the raspberries, icing sugar and 1½ tablespoons of elderflower cordial into a blender and whizz until combined and smoothie-like in texture. Pass the mixture through a sieve into a bowl to get rid of the seeds. Tweak to your liking: add more elderflower if you wish, or icing sugar if you feel it's too sharp. Personally, I find this is just right. Put to one side.

3. When the fruit is cooked let it cool for 5 minutes before handling, as it can be pretty hot from the sugar syrup. Halve the peaches and pears and remove the stones and cores.

4. Put a peach and pear half on each plate and top with some vanilla ice cream, bashed meringue nest, a good drizzle of the raspberry sauce and hazelnuts sprinkled over. Gorgeous!

♟ VIRGIN TIP
I like to eat the fruit with the skin on. But if you prefer the skin removed, it will come off much more easily once you have poached the fruit.

BANANA AND BLUEBERRY BAKEWELL

Bakewell tart has to be up there as one of my most favourite recipes. This twist uses a combination of blueberries and bananas in the filling and base – it works a charm and tastes absolutely delicious slightly warm with some ice cream or custard.

READY IN 45 MINUTES
SERVES 8

1 sheet of ready-rolled shortcrust
    pastry
70g unsalted butter
70g caster sugar
1 large egg
100g ground almonds
1 tbsp plain flour
1 tsp baking powder
2 bananas, mashed
3 tbsp blueberry jam
handful of flaked almonds

TO SERVE
handful of blueberries
icing sugar

1. Preheat the oven to 190°C/170°C fan/375°F/Gas mark 5.

2. Unroll the pastry and use it to line a 23cm loose-bottomed flan tin, pressing the pastry firmly into the tin. Prick the base with a fork, line with baking parchment and fill with baking beans. Blind bake for 12–15 minutes, or until light golden and dry to touch. Remove from the oven and put to one side to cool.

3. Meanwhile, put the butter and sugar into a large bowl and beat together with a hand-held electric whisk until combined. Now add the egg, ground almonds, flour, baking powder and bananas, then whisk well until all merged together into a batter.

4. Spread the blueberry jam over the base of the pastry case, making sure you go right to the edge. Carefully spread the batter over the top until even. Sprinkle over some flaked almonds and bake in the oven for 25 minutes, or until golden brown on top.

5. Allow to cool slightly before finishing with blueberries on top and a dusting of icing sugar. I also like to mix 90g of icing sugar with a few teaspoons of water and drizzle an icing on top.

🎩 **VIRGIN TIP**
If you want to make your own shortcrust pastry (which isn't as hard as you might think), there are several videos on my website, or see page 19.

Goodness, where shall I start here? This chapter is full to the brim with 22 different cakes, bakes and puddings to try; you may need to get some friends round to help you out with some of these. Let's just say that when I was testing these recipes, there sure were a lot of friends dropping in 'by coincidence'.

From delicious custard-stuffed éclairs, quirky shortbreads and cookies, through a no-bake bounty tart (which I think is in my top ten recipes for simplicity), to vodka Jaffa cakes and salted caramel fondant, we've got you covered here. It's just a case of which one you start with!

I'm really excited to see you guys try these sweet treats and bakes. Do let me know how you get on and please send me your pictures . . . and spare slices if you have any.

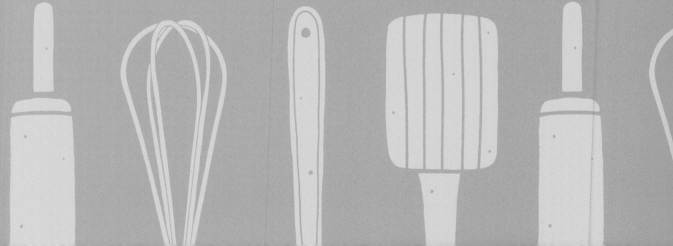

6.
BAKES
& CAKES

PISTACHIO, LAVENDER & HONEY FRIANDS

This recipe reminds me of the summer; the colourful combination of the lavender, honey and pistachios, as well as the gorgeous aroma really makes this a special recipe. Friands are essentially small cakes that originated in France, almost like a shrunken muffin in appearance. Drenching these in an extra lick of honey just before serving is tongue-tinglingly good!

READY IN 15 MINUTES,
PLUS CHILLING TIME
MAKES 12

140g unsalted butter
1½ tbsp dried lavender, plus
    a few buds to decorate
35g plain flour
100g ground almonds
125g icing sugar
50g pistachios, finely chopped,
    plus extra to decorate
4 large egg whites
4 tbsp honey

🎩 **VIRGIN TIP**
Kept in a sealed container, these
little cakes will keep for up to 3 days.

1. Melt the butter in a small saucepan. Gently crush the lavender with your hands to release the fragrance and add to the butter. Cook over a medium-high heat until the butter foams and the milk solids turn a golden brown. Immediately remove from the heat and pour into a bowl.

2. Put the flour, almonds, sugar and pistachios into a large bowl and mix together. Using a hand-held electric whisk, beat the egg whites in a separate bowl to soft peaks. Gently mix the egg whites into the flour until smooth.

3. Strain the butter, discarding the lavender, and gently incorporate into the cake mix until smooth and fully combined. Cover the mixture and refrigerate for an hour before baking.

4. When you're ready to bake preheat the oven to 180°C/160°C fan/350°F/Gas mark 4 and lightly grease a 12-hole non-stick muffin tin.

5. Divide the batter evenly between the prepared muffin holes and bake for 20–25 minutes, or until golden brown around the edges. Allow to cool for a few minutes before turning out on to a wire rack. While they are still warm paint the top of each friand with some honey, dripping it into any cracks in the top. Sprinkle over some extra chopped pistachios and a few lavender buds.

6. When they are cool and you are ready to serve, drizzle a little more honey over the top of each friand.

S'MORE CHEESECAKE

I first discovered s'mores across the pond, sitting around a campfire, although you can make them indoors too (I've done a video on this – check it out). They have become a real hit at home – we even had them at our wedding as favours! The combination of graham crackers (or digestives in the UK), marshmallows and chocolate is a true winner. Here we turn a s'more into a cheesecake: the marshmallow element in the cheesecake filling gets doubled up with a toasty mallow finish!

**READY IN 25 MINUTES,
PLUS CHILLING TIME
SERVES 10**

FOR THE BASE
250g digestive biscuits
110g unsalted butter, melted

FOR THE FILLING
400g marshmallows
70ml semi-skimmed milk
400g cream cheese
250ml double cream, whipped

FOR THE TOPPING
100g milk or plain chocolate chips
150ml double cream
large handful of marshmallows, for
    toasting (or use marshmallow fluff)

♟ VIRGIN TIP
Marshmallow fluff is a great replacement for toasted marshmallow as a way to finish your cheesecake and is available in most supermarkets. Warm up a jar in the microwave or let it sit in hot water for a minute to soften, then drizzle over the cheesecake.

1. First make the no-bake base. Bash the digestive biscuits in a sealed bag with a rolling pin until fine crumbs are achieved. Tip into a bowl, add the melted butter, then mix well to combine. Press this mixture into the base of a 23cm loose-bottomed cake tin but also work the mixture up the sides. Sit in the fridge for the time being to firm up.

2. For the marshmallow filling heat the milk and marshmallows together in a saucepan over a low heat, stirring continuously in order to prevent the mallow sticking to the bottom of the pan. When the marshmallows have merged with the milk, remove from the heat to cool slightly. Once cooled pour into a bowl with the cream cheese and fold through until combined, then fold in the whipped cream, again until combined. Take the biscuit base out of the fridge and pour the topping into it and level off. Return to the fridge for 4 hours to firm up.

3. For the topping put the chocolate chips in a heatproof bowl. Warm the cream in a saucepan over a low heat until just before it comes to the boil. Remove from the heat and pour over the chocolate chips. Stir gently to melt the chocolate chips and keep stirring until you have a smooth ganache.

4. Drizzle lines of the ganache topping all over the cheesecake. Using bamboo skewers toast marshmallows carefully over your gas hob one at a time, carefully blowing them out after they char and catch, then stick them into the ganache. If you can't do this or toast them outside, use marshmallow fluff (see Tip).

HAZELNUT & MAPLE BACON COOKIES

A combination of hazelnut and bacon in a cookie is a little unheard of, but once you make these you'll see why it works. There's definitely an autumnal vibe going on with these lovely soft cookies, which you can whip up in a flash.

READY IN 45 MINUTES
MAKES 18

8 rashers of streaky bacon, fat trimmed
100ml maple syrup, plus extra for the
    bacon and serving
110g unsalted butter
200g soft light brown sugar
1 large egg, beaten
1 tsp vanilla extract
250g plain flour
1 tsp bicarbonate of soda
100g blanched hazelnuts, bashed
    roughly

♙ VIRGIN TIP
The nuts and bacon in this recipe are optional, so you can leave either or both out if you want. I sometimes bash the nuts roughly in a sealed bag before adding them to the mixture. Play around with it and put your own spin on the recipe.

1. Preheat the oven to 180°C/160°C fan/350°F/Gas mark 4 and line a couple of baking sheets with baking parchment, as well as a smaller baking tray.

2. Lay the bacon on the lined tray and use a pastry brush to spread some maple syrup over all the rashers. Bake for 15 minutes, then remove the tray, carefully turn the bacon over with some tongs, give another brush of maple syrup and return to the oven for another 10 minutes, or until fully cooked through. Remove from the oven and put to one side to cool (leave the oven on). When it's cool enough to handle, chop the bacon into fine pieces with a sharp knife and put to one side.

3. Meanwhile make the cookie dough. Cream together the butter and sugar until light and smooth, then add the egg and vanilla extract and beat again to combine. Sift in the flour and bicarbonate of soda and fold through with a metal spoon. Follow up with the hazelnuts and pieces of bacon, again folding through until completely mixed in.

4. Put heaped spoonfuls of the mixture on to the lined baking sheets. They will spread out during baking so space them well apart. Bake for about 10 minutes, or until just starting to brown around the edges. Remove from the oven, allow them to cool for a couple of minutes, then transfer to a wire rack. Brush maple syrup on top just before serving.

GIANT
DIGESTIVE

Ah, the humble digestive biscuit . . . This is another recipe I've had tons of requests for but I saved it for the book and, of course, couldn't resist making a giant version! The digestive dough can just as easily be rolled out thin and turned into smaller, more typical digestives, but hey, why not make a big one for a birthday or get-together? After all, sharing is caring!

**READY IN 30 MINUTES,
PLUS COOLING TIME
MAKES 1 GIANT DIGESTIVE**

250g wholemeal flour, plus extra
    for dusting
220g porridge oats
50g soft light brown sugar
½ tsp bicarbonate of soda
pinch of salt
180g unsalted butter, at room
    temperature
3–4 tbsp milk

1. Preheat the oven to 180°C/160°C fan/350°F/Gas mark 4.

2. Put all the dry ingredients into a large bowl and mix briefly. Rub in the butter with your fingers and thumbs until it has been incorporated into the dry ingredients and resembles breadcrumbs; keep going until you have a consistent texture. Pour in a couple of tablespoons of the milk and mix in the bowl to form a dough. Keep adding as much milk as you need until you have a dough that is soft but not too wet.

3. Get the largest baking sheet you have and line it neatly with baking parchment. Take the parchment out for the moment and sit the ball of dough on it. Use a floured rolling pin to roll the dough out into as large a circle as you can, taking up the full width of the baking parchment.

4. Lift the parchment and biscuit dough on to the tray and bake for 20–22 minutes. Do not over-bake the biscuit; it will firm up once cooked and you do not want it to be like a rock! So start checking after 20 minutes; you may just see it starting to brown around the edges.

5. Transfer to a wire rack to cool before dividing up and sharing with a very large cup of tea!

♛ **VIRGIN TIP**
Melt some dark or milk chocolate after the biscuit has cooled and pour it over the top to turn this into a good old chocolate digestive!

MOCHA BISCUITS

These simple, coffee flavoured biscuits are fun to make and are sandwiched together with melted chocolate – always a good way of eating two biscuits in one!

**READY IN 15 MINUTES,
PLUS COOLING TIME
MAKES 10**

170g unsalted butter, softened
60g icing sugar
180g plain flour
2 tsp coffee granules, dissolved
    in 1 tbsp milk

TO FILL AND DECORATE
150g milk chocolate, melted
150g white chocolate, melted

1. Preheat the oven to 180°C/160°C fan/350°F/Gas mark 4 and line a baking sheet with baking parchment.

2. Cream together the butter and sugar using a hand-held electric whisk. Sift in the flour and fold through with a metal spoon until combined. Add the coffee and milk mixture to the batter and stir until completely combined.

3. Take rounded teaspoons of the dough, and place on the baking sheet, spaced about 2cm apart. Bake for 10–12 minutes, or until just starting to brown and slightly firm on top. Transfer to a wire rack to cool completely.

4. To assemble the biscuits, take one biscuit and turn it upside down with the flat side facing up. Spoon a small quantity of milk or white chocolate into the centre and gently press another biscuit on top so the chocolate holds the biscuit together. Use the other chocolate to zigzag lines over the top of the biscuit for decoration.

5. Keep going until you have sandwiched all the biscuits, alternating with milk or white chocolate for the filling and decoration. Chill in the fridge to allow the chocolate to fully set before eating.

♟ **VIRGIN TIP**
Another option is to dunk the ends of the cooled biscuits in the melted chocolate instead of sandwiching them together – you could even try marbling them!

TOFFEE APPLE PIE

I think the title has probably sold this recipe to you already. This, folks, is a gorgeous apple pie, crammed full of apples and baked with a homemade toffee sauce (keep a little back for drenching slices when it comes to serving time).

READY IN 45 MINUTES
SERVES 8

500g block of ready-made shortcrust pastry (or make your own)

300ml double cream

100g butter

100g soft light brown sugar

5 large Bramley apples, peeled, cored and sliced into small chunks

25g plain flour, plus extra for dusting

1 tbsp ground cinnamon

80g caster sugar, plus extra for dusting (optional)

1 egg, beaten

VIRGIN TIP
If you don't have enough pastry to make a lid you could make a lattice-style topping using woven strips of pastry.

1. Preheat the oven to 190°C/170°C fan/375°F/Gas mark 5.

2. Divide the pastry into two pieces; you will need roughly two-thirds for the base of the pie and the rest for the lid. Using a floured rolling pin, roll out the larger piece of pastry on a floured work surface to about the thickness of a £1 coin. Lift the pastry into a 25cm pie dish and press into the base and up the sides (leave any overhanging edges for now). Roll out the remaining piece of pastry so it is big enough to form the lid and put to one side.

3. Now for the toffee sauce. Pour the double cream, butter and sugar into a saucepan and place over a low heat, stirring until the ingredients melt and combine together. When they are a consistent toffee colour, remove from the heat and transfer to a jug.

4. Put the chopped apples into a bowl with the flour, cinnamon and caster sugar, stirring until they are all coated, then tip into the pastry-lined pie dish. Be sure to fill all the space as the apples will reduce down when cooked. With the pie filled, pour half of the toffee sauce over the apples. Place the pastry lid on top of the pie and press down to seal the edges. Crimp around the edges, using a fork or your fingers, then cut away any excess pastry. Give the top a brush with the beaten egg and sprinkle on extra sugar if you wish.

5. Put the pie dish on a large baking tray (some of the toffee will try to escape so this will catch any drips) and bake for 35–40 minutes until golden brown on top, but keep your eye on it. Allow to cool for a good 15 minutes before serving warm or, as we prefer it, cold with ice cream and some of the leftover toffee sauce warmed up alongside.

STRAWBERRY &
MASCARPONE TARTS

A deliciously simple dessert that can be ready in a flash. These chocolate-dipped strawberries nestling on a bed of mascarpone and golden puff pastry look pretty flashy too so this is a great one to have up your sleeve.

READY IN 20 MINUTES
SERVES 4

1 x 320g sheet of ready-rolled
    puff pastry
1 egg, beaten
250g mascarpone
1 tbsp icing sugar, plus extra for
    dusting
1 tsp vanilla extract
16 strawberries, leafy tops sliced off
100g plain chocolate, melted

1. Preheat the oven to 190°C/170°C fan/375°F/Gas mark 5 and line a baking sheet with baking parchment.

2. Take your sheet of puff pastry and cut it into four rectangles. One at a time score a 1cm border around the edge of each rectangle, leaving enough room to comfortably fit four strawberries. The scored area will become your crusts. Use a fork to prick the area inside the border then give the entire rectangle a brush with the beaten egg wash. Repeat this with all the rectangles.

3. Transfer to the lined baking sheet and bake for 12–15 minutes, or until golden brown. Leave to cool on a wire rack for a few minutes. The middle sections you scored may have risen too; if so use a sharp knife to go over the scored lines again and gently push the middle section down.

4. Meanwhile, in a mixing bowl mix together the mascarpone, sugar and vanilla extract. Spread even amounts of this mixture into the centres of the cooled pastry rectangles, smoothing it out to level off.

5. Dunk the fat ends of the strawberries into the melted chocolate about one-third of the way up and sit inside the pastry pointy side up, four in each tart. Drizzle more melted chocolate with your spoon back and forth over the tarts and give a final dusting of icing sugar. A perfect balance of crunchy pastry, creamy sweetened mascarpone and chocolate-dunked strawberries in one bite!

👨‍🍳 **VIRGIN TIP**
The egg wash is optional, but it really does produce a lovely golden brown colour on the top of the pastry. Try mixing this up with other fruit such as bananas, which work well with the chocolate, or an alternative filling could be blueberries tossed with a little lemon zest.

APPLE, RAISIN & OAT COOKIES

These are quite simply some of the nicest cookies I've ever made. Eating them while still slightly warm from the oven is the best, the combo of warm, soft and mildly chewy cookies is very comforting indeed.

READY IN 15 MINUTES, PLUS COOLING TIME
MAKES 18

140g unsalted butter, at room temperature
100g soft light brown sugar
50g granulated sugar
1 egg
1 tsp vanilla extract
140g plain flour
½ tsp ground cinnamon
½ tsp nutmeg
½ tsp bicarbonate of soda
150g porridge oats
2 apples, peeled, cored and cut into small pieces
150g raisins
2 tbsp milk

1. Preheat the oven to 180°C/160°C fan/350°F/Gas mark 4 and line a couple of baking sheets with baking parchment.

2. In a mixing bowl cream together the butter and sugars using a hand-held electric whisk until light and fluffy. Whisk in the egg and vanilla extract and then sift in the flour, cinnamon, nutmeg and bicarbonate of soda and fold through until the mixture has thickened slightly and all the flour is incorporated into the mixture.

3. Add the porridge oats, apple pieces and raisins, mixing through well with a spoon to combine. The mixture should be pretty stiff by now, so add the milk and mix through to make it easier to handle.

4. With clean hands roll the cookie dough into golf ball size portions and place on the lined baking sheets, spacing about 2–3cm apart. Bake for 10–12 minutes, or until just starting to brown around the edges. Transfer to a wire rack to cool, although I think these are best when still slightly warm . . . enjoy!

🎩 **VIRGIN TIP**
Mix these up even more by adding other dried fruits such as cranberries, or other spices such as mixed spice – delicious!

JAFFA WHOOPIE PIES

Whoopie pies, or chocolate burgers as Chloe calls them, are extremely soft, cream-filled cakes that we discovered in Cape Cod. The one we had could have fed the four of us and if you make these you'll see why. The buttermilk helps to create a delicate soft sponge that when sandwiched together with tangy marmalade and orange buttercream is a winning combo!

READY IN 30 MINUTES
MAKES 8

120g unsalted butter, softened
200g soft light brown sugar
1 large egg, beaten
45g cocoa powder
350g plain flour
1 tsp bicarbonate of soda
250ml buttermilk

FOR THE ORANGE BUTTERCREAM

250g unsalted butter, softened
500g icing sugar
1 tbsp orange extract
zest and juice of ½ orange

TO ASSEMBLE

orange marmalade

♛ VIRGIN TIP
You can mix the batter by hand but you'll need a fair amount of elbow grease; if you don't fancy a workout an electric whisk or stand mixer is highly recommended.

1. Preheat the oven to 180°C/160°C fan/350°F/Gas mark 4 and line a couple of baking sheets with baking parchment.

2. Put the butter and sugar into a large bowl and cream together using a hand-held electric whisk until fully incorporated. Add the egg and whisk again. Sift in the cocoa powder, flour and bicarbonate of soda with the buttermilk and mix together really well. You want the batter as smooth as possible so add in batches if you prefer. The batter will be quite thick once ready.

3. Dollop 16 tablespoons of the batter on to the lined baking sheets – well spaced out as they expand considerably! If the tops are a little rough wet your finger and smooth them down. Bake for about 12 minutes; the tops of the pies should still be a little soft and springy (you don't want a crust on top like when making muffins). Remove from the oven and transfer to a wire rack to cool completely.

4. Meanwhile, make the buttercream by beating together the butter and sugar until smooth. Add the orange extract, orange zest and juice and mix through well to combine. Leave to one side.

5. When the pies are fully cooled take a half for the bottom of a pie (you can press it down a little or take a small slice from the bottom if it does not sit level on a surface), spread a little marmalade on the flat side and then spread some buttercream on top. Grab another half and spread with another thin layer of marmalade, then press lightly on top of the bottom half. Repeat until you have a lovely batch of choco orange pies. Let the buttercream settle before eating. Store in an airtight container for up to 5 days.

VODKA JAFFA CAKES

Who doesn't love Jaffa cakes? Making your own from scratch is pretty easy indeedy. We are taking them up a notch here to create an adult treat, using a vodka jelly for the centre. Just remember to keep these away from the kids!

**READY IN 30 MINUTES,
PLUS CHILLING TIME
MAKES 12**

135g orange jelly, broken into cubes
150ml boiling water
50ml cold water
100ml vodka
2 large eggs
60g caster sugar
60g plain flour
1 tsp orange extract (optional)
1 tbsp marmalade
200g plain chocolate, broken
   into pieces

🎩 **VIRGIN TIP**
You can reduce the strength of
these by replacing some of the
vodka with cold water (or remove
entirely for a kid-friendly version);
it's all about experimentation. You
could also add orange extract to
the melted chocolate for a further
orange boost.

1. Ideally, make the jelly a few hours ahead or the night before as it needs time to set. Mix the jelly cubes with the boiling water until dissolved, add the cold water (to cool the jelly slightly but maintain the alcohol content) then pour in the vodka, stirring for a moment. Pour the jelly into the bottoms of a muffin tin with 12 very small holes if you have one; if not pour into a small baking tray or dish to a depth of about 1cm. Put in the fridge to set.

2. Preheat the oven to 180°C/160°C fan/350°F/Gas mark 4 and lightly grease the holes of a shallow cupcake tin.

3. Make the sponge by whisking together the eggs with the sugar in a bowl using a hand-held electric whisk until light in colour – this should take a couple of minutes. Add the flour and fold through with a spoon. I like to stir through a little orange extract now, so do this if you want to. Spoon the mixture into the holes of the cupcake tin – you only need to just cover the bottoms as they will rise in the oven slightly. Bake for 10 minutes until cooked through. Allow to cool for a moment, then remove the cakes from the tin and cool fully on a wire rack.

4. While the bases are cooling turn out the jelly circles. If you used a baking tray, cut out circles using a shot glass or do this carefully with a knife.

5. Spoon a tiny quantity of marmalade on the centre of each cake – this is just to give them a little Jaffa boost and to act as a glue to stop the jelly moving. Place a jelly circle on top of each cake and return to the fridge for the moment.

6. Put the chocolate into a heatproof bowl and melt in the microwave in 20-second bursts, stirring until smooth. Let it stand until it is room temperature (test with your finger). You want it manoeuvrable but not so hot that it melts the jelly. Sit the cakes on a wire rack and carefully spoon the chocolate over the tops, letting it drizzle down. Once they are all coated, immediately put in the fridge to firm up. Give them a good hour to set and then get tasting!

GINGER LOAF WITH LIME ICING

I love a good ginger cake. When I was younger I used to have quite a strong dislike of ginger flavour but I believe a ginger sponge changed that. This recipe makes a lovely dense ginger loaf, using a mix of ground and stem ginger along with some mixed spice. The zingy lime icing on top of the loaf is the perfect contrast. I'm pretty sure this will become a favourite once you try it – hope you like it as much as we do!

READY IN 1½ HOURS
SERVES 10-12

100g unsalted butter
100g soft light brown sugar
100g black treacle
100g golden syrup
225ml milk
200g self-raising flour
1 tsp baking powder
1 tsp ground ginger
1 tsp mixed spice
80g stem ginger, very finely chopped
1 large egg, beaten

FOR THE ICING
50g icing sugar
zest of 1 lime, plus the juice of ½

1. Preheat the oven to 180°C/160°C fan/350°F/Gas mark 4 and grease and line a large 23 x 12cm loaf tin with baking parchment.

2. Put the butter, sugar, treacle, syrup and milk into a saucepan and melt over a low heat until the sugar has dissolved. Remove from the heat and set aside to cool.

3. Combine the flour, baking powder and spices in a large bowl. Pour in the treacle mixture and beat with a spatula until smooth. Add the chopped ginger and stir in the beaten egg. The mixture will be a loose batter.

4. Tip the batter into the prepared tin and bake for 1 hour until a skewer comes out clean. Allow to cool in the tin.

5. Make the icing by combining all the ingredients in a bowl and beating until smooth. Once the cake is cool turn out of the tin, peel off the parchment and drizzle over the icing. If you have a spare lime a little extra zest will give a lovely colour contrast on top.

♟ VIRGIN TIP
To make this a bit more special, serve with raspberries marinated in the rest of the lime juice and a teaspoon or two of sugar to taste.

MINTED MILLIONAIRE SHORTBREADS

Millionaire shortbread is something of a classic; with that lovely baked shortbread base, caramel filling and chocolate topping, there's not much to dislike. But if you are a fan of chocolate and mint, this may just take it up a notch – they look great too!

READY IN 40 MINUTES, PLUS CHILLING TIME
MAKES 16

FOR THE BASE
180g plain flour
60g caster sugar
130g unsalted butter, chilled and diced

FOR THE CARAMEL AND TOPPING
2 tbsp golden syrup
50g caster sugar
130g unsalted butter, cut into cubes
400g tin condensed milk
box of mint flavour Matchmakers, chopped roughly
150g milk chocolate
100g white chocolate
1½ tsp mint extract

♟ **VIRGIN TIP**
These are best stored in the fridge – take them out a few minutes before serving and eating.

1. Preheat the oven to 180°C/160°C fan/350°F/Gas mark 4. Line an 18cm square cake tin with baking parchment, or use a silicone tray if you have one.

2. Make the base by rubbing the butter into the sugar and flour using your fingers. After about 5 minutes it should cling together as a dough. Press into the prepared tin and level with your hands. Bake for about 15 minutes until golden brown. Allow to cool.

3. To make the caramel put the golden syrup, sugar, butter and condensed milk into a heavy-based saucepan and stir over a low heat. Stir constantly until the mixture turns a darker colour and thickens to a custard texture. Do not cook it too long or it will burn; 10 minutes is about right, but keep an eye on it. Carefully tip this mixture over the base; it should level out itself.

4. Let the caramel cool for about 5 minutes. It will firm up as it cools, so sprinkle over half the Matchmakers so they stick to the caramel before it gets too firm but the heat won't melt them.

5. Meanwhile, melt the chocolates in separate heatproof bowls set over a pan of just simmering water (make sure the bottom of the bowl doesn't touch the water). Or if you have a microwave, melt it in 20-second bursts, stirring between each one.

6. Stir the mint extract through the milk chocolate then pour over the caramel layer. Let it settle then stick in the remaining Matchmakers. Drizzle the white chocolate over in a zigzag pattern.

7. Put in the fridge for 45 minutes to firm up and set then remove and cut into portions (I'll leave the size up to you!).

PEACHES & CREAM 'TRES LECHES' BUNDT CAKE

A 'tres leches' cake is essentially a classic sponge soaked in three types of milk – cream, condensed milk and evaporated milk. The technique involves poking holes in the cake and letting it absorb the milky mixture after baking. The Bundt shape gives the perfect opportunity to fill the centre with whatever ingredients you choose; I think peaches work a charm, but you could also use nuts.

**READY IN 50 MINUTES,
PLUS 2 HOURS CHILLING TIME
SERVES 12**

6 large eggs, separated
¼ tsp baking powder
¼ tsp salt
220g caster sugar
115g unsalted butter, melted
150g self-raising flour, sifted
180ml evaporated milk
120ml single cream
180ml condensed milk

TO SERVE
4 ripe peaches, peeled and sliced

♕ VIRGIN TIP
This cake is great with strawberries too. Hull and quarter them before adding to the cake for a strawberries and cream vibe.

1. Preheat the oven to 180°C/160°C fan/350°F/Gas mark 4 and grease a 24cm Bundt tin.

2. Use a hand-held electric whisk to beat the egg whites vigorously in a large bowl. Once they start to stiffen add the baking powder and salt and beat until soft peaks form. Reduce the speed of the mixer and add the egg yolks, one at a time, and sugar. Continue mixing until smooth.

3. Use a spatula to fold in the melted butter then carefully fold in the flour in 3 or 4 batches until the mixture is well combined. Pour the mixture into the prepared tin and bake for 35–40 minutes until it is well risen and springs back when you gently press the top. While the cake is still hot and in its tin, poke lots of holes all over it with a skewer. Make the holes deep and close together.

4. Beat together the evaporated milk, cream and condensed milk. Pour half of the mixture over the cake, little by little, giving it time to sink in before adding more. Put the tin in the fridge for 2 hours to chill.

5. After 2 hours loosen the cake by sliding a palette knife around the edges as far as possible. To turn the cake out, use a chopping board that completely covers the Bundt tin. Hold the board tightly over the tin then invert it and sharply bang the board and tin on the work surface to release the cake. You may need to give it a couple of bangs before the cake drops out. Once the cake is out of the tin transfer it to a wide serving plate with a lipped edge.

6. Poke more holes in the cake and pour over half of the remaining cream mixture. Fill the centre hole of the cake with fresh peach slices; chop the remaining slices into chunks and scatter over the top and around the edges. Chill in the fridge until you're ready to eat.

7. Drizzle the cake and peaches with the remaining cream and serve.

NO-BAKE BOUNTY TART

This is one of the easiest but most impressive looking recipes in the whole book. If you are a fan of Bounty bars (a.k.a. Mounds in the USA) and are after a dessert that will be a hit with very little preparation, this is it. A no-bake biscuit base, Bounty-esque filling and chocolate layer topped with toasted coconut. Simple but dreamy.

READY IN 20 MINUTES, PLUS CHILLING TIME
SERVES 12

250g digestive biscuits
170g unsalted butter, melted
400g tin condensed milk
250g desiccated coconut
200g plain chocolate, broken
    into pieces

🍳 VIRGIN TIP
If you prefer you can bake the crust before filling – just use the same recipe and bake in an oven preheated to 170°C/150°C fan/325°F/ Gas mark 3 for 8–10 minutes, or until golden brown. You could also use toasted coconut for the filling as well as the topping.

1. Preheat the oven to 170°C/150°C fan/325°F/Gas mark 3 and line a baking sheet with baking paper.

2. Put the digestive biscuits into a sealable bag and bash with a rolling pin until you have fine crumbs. Tip the crumbs into a large bowl, add the melted butter and stir with a spatula to completely coat the crumbs. Press into a 23cm loose-bottomed flan tin, pressing down to make sure the base is smooth and compact and pushing up the sides as well to create a crust.

3. Pour the condensed milk and 200g of the desiccated coconut into a separate bowl and mix well until thickened and combined; it should have a little bit of movement in it. Push the mixture on to the biscuit base and, using a spatula, carefully spread it evenly to the sides all the way round, making sure the top is nice and level. Put in the fridge for the moment.

4. Scatter the remaining coconut on the lined baking sheet and toast for about 8 minutes, but keep your eye on it as it can catch very quickly. Remove from the oven and put to one side to cool.

5. Put the chocolate into a heatproof bowl. Melt it, either by setting the bowl over a pan of just simmering water (a bain marie) or melt in the microwave in 20-second bursts. Stir until smooth. Carefully pour the chocolate mixture over the coconut, again spreading out to the sides to cover the filling. Finish by sprinkling the toasted coconut on top of the chocolate.

6. Put in the fridge for at least 1 hour to firm up before cutting into slices.

OREO & ROLO BLONDIES

A deliciously naughty treat. Blondies are the lesser-known alternative to brownies, but just as naughty! Here we add some confectionery favourites to the mix: Oreos in the blondie batter and Rolos stuffed inside, oozing a chocolate and caramel layer into the final baked treat! Have one of these, give the rest to friends, then go for a massive run afterwards to make up for it!

**READY IN 40 MINUTES,
PLUS COOLING TIME
MAKES 12**

200g unsalted butter, melted
200g soft light brown sugar
100g caster sugar
2 large eggs, beaten
1 tsp vanilla extract
250g plain flour
½ tsp baking powder
12 Oreos, bashed roughly with
   a rolling pin in a sealable bag
10 Rolos

1. Preheat the oven to 180°C/160°C fan/350°F/Gas mark 4 and lightly grease an 18cm square cake tin.

2. Cream together the butter, sugars, eggs and vanilla extract in a large bowl until fully combined. Fold through the flour and baking powder, then stir in the Oreo chunks.

3. Pour half of the mixture into the prepared tin, then scatter the Rolos on top. Pour the remaining batter over the top to hide the Rolos. Make sure the mixture is fully levelled out, then bake in the oven for 20–25 minutes, or until the top is lightly browned and a skewer inserted into the middle comes out clean.

4. Remove from the oven to cool before slicing up into blondie blocks and serving. These are also great after being chilled in the fridge so the filling firms up.

🍳 **VIRGIN TIP**
Although it is tempting, do not go over the top by adding more Rolos; too much filling in the middle can merge into the base layer. It'll still taste great but it won't be very stable!

SALTED CARAMEL FONDANT PUDDINGS

One of my ultimate guilty pleasures is a good fondant pudding: the sight of that gorgeous filling oozing out is one to behold and very satisfying indeed when you get it right! These salted caramel puddings work a charm and make you feel pretty proud – the caramel is made from scratch so you can make it as salty (or not) as you like. Keep any leftover caramel sauce and serve over ice cream, with pancakes or as a dip for fruit skewers. This is a special dessert for a special occasion for two, but you could easily double it up to serve four.

READY IN 40 MINUTES
SERVES 2

FOR THE CARAMEL SAUCE

125g caster sugar
70ml double cream
25g unsalted butter
Maldon sea salt, to taste

FOR THE PUDDINGS

62g unsalted butter, at room
    temperature, plus extra for greasing
62g soft light brown sugar
1 large egg
50g self-raising flour
12g cocoa powder

TO SERVE

vanilla ice cream or cream

1. To make the caramel sauce, tip the sugar into a heavy-based saucepan, stir in 2 tablespoons of water, then place over a medium heat until the sugar has dissolved. Turn up the heat and bubble for 45 minutes until you have a caramel. Remove from the heat, then carefully stir in the cream and butter; it may splutter so be careful. Carefully pour the sauce into a bowl, allow to cool, then cover and chill in the fridge to set.

2. Preheat the oven to 180°C/160°C fan/350°F/Gas mark 4 and thoroughly butter two 180ml pudding moulds. Put a small circle of baking parchment in the bottom of each one and put them in the fridge while you make the cake mix.

3. Whisk together the butter and sugar in a bowl until fluffy, then whisk in the egg and gently fold in the flour and cocoa. Take the moulds out of the fridge and give them another thin coating of butter.

4. Fill the moulds two-thirds full with the cake mixture. Make a dip in the centre and carefully spoon 1 teaspoon of the set caramel into each and sprinkle with a few flakes of Maldon salt. Gently top up the moulds with the remaining mixture, taking care not to squidge the caramel sauce out.

5. Put the moulds on a baking tray and bake for 20–23 minutes until they are starting to come away from the edge of the mould. Leave to stand for 1 minute then turn the puddings out on to serving plates. Peel off the parchment and serve with a scoop of vanilla ice cream and an extra drizzle of caramel sauce, which can be reheated either in a saucepan or microwave.

♕ VIRGIN TIP

When topping up the moulds with cake mixture, try starting at the edges. If you dollop on top of the caramel centre it's likely to squidge out to the sides. It will still be delicious but you might not get an oozy centre.

PASSION FRUIT MERINGUE CAKE

A totally tropical meringue cake that will really impress friends and family, especially all the surprise elements! We've got layers of sponge, meringue, cream and fruit going on here. It's a really fun cake to make that is a little different – check out those cheeky hidden elements of coconut and lime.

**READY IN 1 HOUR,
PLUS COOLING TIME
SERVES 10-12**

120g unsalted butter, softened
120g caster sugar
2 large eggs
120g self-raising flour

FOR THE MERINGUE

4 medium egg whites
200g caster sugar
50g desiccated coconut

FOR THE FILLING

500ml double cream
2 passion fruit, juice and seeds
½ ripe mango, peeled and chopped
toasted coconut and lime zest,
    to decorate

1. Preheat the oven to 190°C/170°C fan/375°F/Gas mark 5 and butter and line 2 x 20cm sandwich tins with baking parchment.

2. Whisk together the butter and sugar until light and fluffy. Beat in the eggs then gently fold in the flour. Divide the mixture between the tins and gently spread to the edges.

3. Whisk the egg whites in a spotlessly clean bowl to soft peaks. Slowly add the sugar, a spoonful at a time, whisking between each addition. Stir in the desiccated coconut. Spoon the meringue mixture over the cake batter, spread out evenly and make it fairly flat. Bake in the oven for 20–25 minutes. Then remove from the oven and allow to cool in the tin for a while. The meringue will deflate a bit. Use a knife to loosen the edges then turn out to cool completely, removing the baking parchment from the bottom.

4. Softly whip the cream and swirl through two-thirds of the passion fruit pulp. Once completely cold, lay one cake, meringue side up, on a serving plate. Spoon over half of the cream and gently spread to the edges. Arrange half of the mango pieces on top. Put the second layer, cake side down, on top then spread the remaining cream over and top with the remaining mango. Sprinkle with extra coconut and some lime zest to decorate.

🎩 **VIRGIN TIP**
If you don't like mango keep the tropical vibe going by switching up to an alternative ingredient such as pineapple – yummy!

CARROT CAKE CUPCAKES

Of all the recipes I have been testing for this book this is, without doubt, one of Mrs Barry's favourites. The nuts are optional, but they really add to the texture and work brilliantly with the jam topping. Warning: these are highly addictive.

READY IN 30 MINUTES, PLUS COOLING TIME
MAKES 16

180ml vegetable oil
220g soft light brown sugar
4 large eggs
100g wholemeal self-raising flour
1 tsp nutmeg
1 tsp bicarbonate of soda
25g chopped walnuts (optional), plus extra for topping
25g salted peanuts, bashed into rough chunks (optional)
180g (about 2 medium) carrots, grated

FOR THE JAM TOPPING
4 tbsp strawberry jam
zest and juice of 1 lemon

1. Preheat the oven to 180°C/160°C fan/350°F/Gas mark 4 and line a couple of cupcake tins with paper cases.

2. Put the vegetable oil and sugar into a large bowl and use a hand-held electric whisk to mix together until well combined. Crack in the eggs one at a time, whisking between each addition. Now sift in the flour, nutmeg and bicarbonate of soda and fold through with a metal spoon until incorporated. Fold in the nuts, if using, then add the grated carrot and stir until mixed in.

3. Fill each cupcake case half-full with the mixture. Bake in the oven for 25 minutes, or until browned and risen. Check with a skewer – they are ready if it comes out clean – then transfer to a wire rack to cool completely.

4. While the cupcakes are baking, warm the jam in a bowl in the microwave in 15-second bursts (or in a saucepan over a low heat), stirring as you go until it is just warmed through. Stir in the lemon juice.

5. Top the cupcakes with the jam mixture, spreading out to fully coat the tops. Decorate with a few pieces of chopped walnut and sprinkle with lemon zest.

♟ VIRGIN TIP
Don't be alarmed if the batter is not as thick as you would normally expect; this is because it uses oil instead of butter, resulting in cupcakes with a light, airy feel to them.

PINEAPPLE AND LIME POTS

These pots combine the flavours of pineapple, mint and lime for a truly tropical vibe. Make these ahead and chill until needed; they make a great after-dinner treat and the steps are pretty hassle-free too.

READY IN 20 MINUTES, PLUS CHILLING TIME SERVES 4

9 tinned pineapple rings in juice
180ml boiling water
6g powdered gelatine
zest and juice of 2 limes
180g reduced-fat cream cheese
400g tin condensed milk
few sprigs of mint

1. Put a griddle pan over a medium heat. Drain the pineapple rings, reserving a tablespoon of juice. Cook the pineapple rings in batches in the griddle pan for 1–2 minutes on both sides until lightly charred. Repeat until all the pineapple rings are charred. Finely slice two of the pineapple rings and place to one side; put the rest of the pineapple rings into a blender.

2. Pour the boiling water into a jug and add the gelatine granules; stir through until dissolved, then put to one side to cool.

3. Add half the lime zest and all the lime juice to the blender along with the reserved pineapple juice, cream cheese and condensed milk. Now carefully pour in the slightly cooled gelatine mixture, put the lid on and blitz. After about 30 seconds it should be fully blended so have a little taste; if you want to add more lime or pineapple juice, now is the time to do it.

4. Pour the mixture into four serving pots. Divide the remaining chopped pineapple between the pots and stir through carefully. Top the pots with the leftover lime zest and a sprig of mint. Chill in the fridge for 1 hour at the very least before serving.

🍳 **VIRGIN TIP**
Try mixing this up with other ingredients too, such as mango or lemons.

MALTED PEANUT BUTTER DRIP CAKE

This is a truly epic stack of a cake: three malt-infused sponges with a delicious peanut butter and jam filling. The cake is finished with a final coating of the icing and given a trendy drip effect with a chocolate finish. You can load this cake up to the max and finish it in a variety of ways. It really does taste as good as it looks!

READY IN 1½ HOURS, PLUS COOLING AND SETTING TIME
SERVES 20

360g unsalted butter, softened,
　　plus extra for greasing
360g soft light brown sugar
6 large eggs
320g self-raising flour
40g Ovaltine (malted drink powder)
500g reduced-fat cream cheese
200g smooth peanut butter
200g icing sugar
4 tbsp strawberry jam
180g plain chocolate
100ml double cream
30g butter
chocolates and sprinkles, to decorate

1. Preheat the oven to 180°C/160°C fan/350°F/Gas mark 4 and butter and line the bases of 3 x 20cm sandwich tins with baking parchment.

2. Beat together the butter and brown sugar in a large mixing bowl, using a hand-held electric whisk, until pale and fluffy (this will take a few minutes). Whisk in the eggs, one at a time, then gently fold in the flour and Ovaltine.

3. Divide the mixture evenly between the three tins, gently spreading it to the edges. Bake for 20 minutes until the cakes are risen and golden and spring back when you gently press the centre. Leave to cool in the tins for 10 minutes then ease out, remove the baking parchment and cool completely on a wire rack.

4. While the cakes are cooling, beat together the cream cheese, peanut butter and icing sugar. Put it in the fridge until you're ready to use it.

5. Once the cakes are cool, put the first layer on a serving plate and spread with 2 tablespoons of jam, right to the edges. Spread 3 tablespoons of the peanut butter icing over the jam, then layer the next sponge cake on top. Repeat the jam and icing on the next layer and top with the final sponge.

6. Cover the sides and top of the cake with a thin layer of the icing, leaving about half the icing in the bowl. This layer will have some crumbs and jam showing through but if you chill the cake for 1 hour, you'll be able to spread the whole cake again with another, smoother layer of icing. Return to the fridge.

7. Put the chocolate, cream and butter into a heatproof bowl and set over a saucepan of simmering water (making sure the bottom of the bowl doesn't touch the water). Let the mixture cool a little until it's a consistency that will drip down the sides of the cake but not run off. When you're ready to drip, take the cake out of the fridge and start with the drips around the edge, working your way round so you have drips and dribbles down the cake at uneven points. Once the edges are done, fill in the centre and smooth over. If the chocolate has started to set a little too much, warm your palette knife in a cup of hot water and dry before smoothing over the top of the cake.

8. Before the chocolate sets arrange chocolates, sweets and sprinkles on top. It looks great if you make the highest point slightly off centre. Return to the fridge to completely set before serving.

MOCHA CUSTARD ÉCLAIRS

'Blimey' was Mrs Barry's expression after we'd finished testing these creamy, custard-filled homemade éclairs drenched in a speedy mocha icing. These can be as simple or as complex as you want them to be.

READY IN 50 MINUTES
SERVES 8

FOR THE CHOUX PASTRY

100g unsalted butter
1 tsp vanilla extract
150g plain flour
pinch of salt
4 large eggs

FOR THE CUSTARD CREAM

250ml whole milk
2 tbsp custard powder
2 tbsp sugar
250ml double cream, whipped
   to soft peaks

FOR THE MOCHA ICING

1 tsp coffee granules
1 tsp cocoa powder
150g icing sugar

1. First prepare the choux pastry. Preheat the oven to 190°C/170°C fan/375°F/Gas mark 5 and line a large baking sheet with baking parchment. Put the butter in a saucepan with 240ml water and the vanilla extract. Place over a low heat and bring to a gentle simmer, stirring until the butter is melted. Remove from the heat and sift in the flour and salt. The mixture will instantly thicken, so keep stirring with a spatula for a couple of minutes until it all comes together like a big clump of Play-Doh. Add the eggs one at a time and beat well into the mixture; keep going and they will eventually merge. When a consistently smooth texture is achieved you have made choux pastry!

2. If you're comfortable with piping, spoon the mixture into a piping bag fitted with a plain round nozzle and pipe 8 x 15cm strips on the lined baking sheet. Alternatively, use a small spoon to spread the mixture in strips. For neat éclairs smooth the tops with a wet finger (although any imperfections will be covered with icing). Sprinkle a few drops of water on the tray to help generate steam.

3. Bake for about 25 minutes until risen, golden brown and crisp; do not open the oven at all during baking or they will collapse. I like to turn the oven off and leave them in there for a few minutes more before removing them. Transfer to a wire rack and make a small incision with a knife to release the steam inside. Leave to cool completely and to dry out the insides.

4. Meanwhile make the filling. Put the milk, custard powder and sugar into a saucepan and place over a medium heat, stirring steadily until the mixture thickens and is looking custard-like in texture. Transfer to a bowl, lay a piece of cling film over the surface (to stop a skin forming) and put to one side to cool to room temperature, then chill in the fridge.

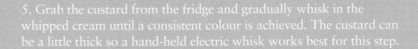

♟ VIRGIN TIP
You can change these to choux buns by dolloping heaped tablespoons of dough on to the baking sheet. Make sure they are fully dried out before filling with the cream.

5. Grab the custard from the fridge and gradually whisk in the whipped cream until a consistent colour is achieved. The custard can be a little thick so a hand-held electric whisk works best for this step.

6. Make a cut along the tops of the éclairs to open them up from one end to the other, pressing back any loose bits of dough internally to the sides. Using a teaspoon, load the éclairs with the custard cream, pushing the cream into as much of the hole as possible to fill them well. Push the tops down gently to encase the custard filling.

7. Mix the coffee granules and cocoa powder with a tablespoon of boiling water in a large bowl until smooth, then sift in the icing sugar. Blend until smooth, adding a little more water if needed – the icing should thickly coat the back of a spoon. Spoon over the tops of the éclairs to fully coat them. Allow the icing to set, then keep in the fridge until ready to gobble up!

MANGO CRÈME BRÛLÉE

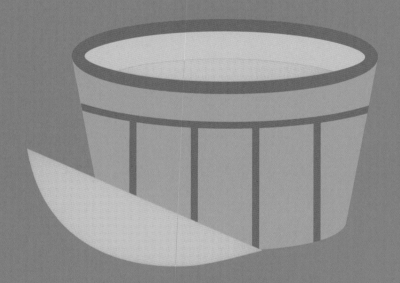

This is one of those desserts I never thought I could make, but crème brûlée is well worth having in your repertoire. It's taken me a few attempts to really crack this recipe, but I'm sure this no-bake version will be very popular. I've given it a mild mango twist that works well with the vanilla. Follow the recipe carefully (I've learned a few tips along the way) and you should be fine.

**READY IN 25 MINUTES,
PLUS CHILLING TIME
SERVES 4**

½ fresh mango, peeled and cut
  into small chunks
1 vanilla pod
600ml double cream
5 large egg yolks
50g caster sugar, plus extra for
  the topping

🎩 **VIRGIN TIP**
If you do not have a chef's blowtorch
put the ramekins on a baking tray
and slide under a grill preheated to
high to caramelise the tops. Keep
your eye on them as the sugar
quickly turns from golden to burnt.
Take care as the bubbling sugar will
be very hot.

1. First get four ramekins and put a few chunks of mango in the bottom of each one, reserving a few small pieces of mango to decorate each finished brûlée (keep these in a container in the fridge).

2. Cut the ends off the vanilla pod, lightly score down the middle to open it out and run the tip of your knife along it to remove the seeds. Put the seeds, the vanilla pod itself and the cream in a saucepan and place over a low heat. Bring the cream towards a simmer, but the moment you see the first trace of bubbles appearing remove from the heat.

3. Meanwhile, beat together the egg yolks and sugar in a separate bowl with a hand-held electric whisk until pale. This should only take a minute or so don't over-beat it. Now switch to a balloon whisk and continue to whisk by hand while you steadily pour the cream into the yolks. Go slowly so that the egg adjusts to the temperature of the cream and keep whisking until everything is combined.

4. Pour the mixture through a sieve into a clean saucepan to remove the pod (the vanilla seeds will slip through but that is fine). Place over a medium heat and slowly bring up to a simmer, continuing to mix with a wooden spoon or spatula. It is essential to stir constantly to keep the cream at a steady temperature. After about 5 minutes you should notice that the consistency is noticeably thicker and a lot more like custard.

5. Remove from the heat and pour into the ramekin dishes on top of the mango layers. Put to one side to come to room temperature, then cover with cling film and chill in the fridge for at least 5 hours, or ideally overnight.

6. When ready to serve remove the ramekins from the fridge and sprinkle a couple of teaspoons of caster sugar over the top of each one. Use a chef's blowtorch to caramelise the sugar until golden brown. Let the sugar cool to harden and serve with the reserved mango on top.

CONVERSION CHARTS

DRY WEIGHTS

METRIC	IMPERIAL	METRIC	IMPERIAL
5g	¼oz	500g	1lb 2oz
8/10g	⅓oz	550g	1lb 3oz
15g	½oz	600g	1lb 5oz
20g	¾oz	625g	1lb 6oz
25g	1oz	650g	1lb 7oz
30/35g	1¼oz	675g	1½lb
40g	1½oz	700g	1lb 9oz
50g	2oz	750g	1lb 10oz
60/70g	2½oz	800g	1¾lb
75/85/90g	3oz	850g	1lb 14oz
100g	3½oz	900g	2lb
110/120g	4oz	950g	2lb 2oz
125/130g	4½oz	1kg	2lb 3oz
135/140/150g	5oz	1.1kg	2lb 6oz
170/175g	6oz	1.25kg	2¾lb
200g	7oz	1.3/1.4kg	3lb
225g	8oz	1.5kg	3lb 5oz
250g	9oz	1.75/1.8kg	4lb
265g	9½oz	2kg	4lb 4oz
275g	10oz	2.25kg	5lb
300g	11oz	2.5kg	5½lb
325g	11½oz	3kg	6½lb
350g	12oz	3.5kg	7¾lb
375g	13oz	4kg	8¾lb
400g	14oz	4.5kg	9¾lb
425g	15oz	6.8kg	15lb
450g	1lb	9kg	20lb
475g	1lb 1oz		

568ml = 1 UK pint (20fl oz) | 16fl oz = 1 US pint

LIQUID MEASURES

METRIC	IMPERIAL	CUPS	METRIC	IMPERIAL	CUPS
15ml	½fl oz	1 tbsp (level)	425ml	15fl oz	
20ml	¾fl oz		450ml	16fl oz	2 cups
25ml	1fl oz	⅛ cup	500ml	18fl oz	2¼ cups
30ml	1¼fl oz		550ml	19fl oz	
50ml	2fl oz	¼ cup	600ml	1 pint	2½ cups
60ml	2½fl oz		700ml	1¼ pints	
75ml	3fl oz		750ml	1⅓ pints	
100ml	3½fl oz	⅜ cup	800ml	1 pint 9fl oz	
110/120ml	4fl oz	½ cup	850ml	1½ pints	
125ml	4½fl oz		900ml	1 pint 12fl oz	3¾ cups
150ml	5fl oz	⅔ cup	1 litre	1¾ pints	1 quart (4 cups)
175ml	6fl oz	¾ cup	1.2 litres	2 pints	1¼ quarts
200/215ml	7fl oz		1.25 litres	2¼ pints	
225ml	8fl oz	1 cup	1.5 litres	2½ pints	3 US pints
250ml	9fl oz		1.75/1.8 litres	3 pints	
275ml	9½fl oz		2 litres	3½ pints	2 quarts
300ml	½ pint	1¼ cups	2.2 litres	3¾ pints	
350ml	12fl oz	1½ cups	2.5 litres	4⅓ pints	
375ml	13fl oz		3 litres	5 pints	
400ml	14fl oz		3.5 litres	6 pints	

OVEN TEMPERATURES

°C	°F	GAS MARK	DESCRIPTION
110	225	¼	cool
130	250	½	cool
140	275	1	very low
150	300	2	very low
160/170	325	3	low to moderate
180	350	4	moderate
190	375	5	moderately hot
200	400	6	hot
220	425	7	hot
230	450	8	hot
240	475	9	very hot

INDEX

THANK YOUS

My wife Becky and daughters Phoebe and Chloe for giving me the confidence, love, support and motivation to do all of this.

Barry Smith, a good friend and mentor.

Allison Clarkson, for helping bring these recipes to life.

Andrew Brown and Natalie for photographing the cover.

Grace, Sarah and all at HarperCollins for supporting me with another amazing book.